MW00618025

Reader Reviews

"I enjoyed the material in the book immensely. The skill set revealed has helped me make huge leaps forward professionally and will greatly affect the trajectory of my career."
Lance Lunsford, Director of Marketing
UMC Health System

"I can't tell you how much I have enjoyed and benefited from *So, What's Your Point?* Several months ago, I submitted myself for consideration for a very high profile position at Beaver Creek Ski Resort. Following an extremely lengthy, competitive and complicated interview process, I was offered the position of Executive Director of the Beaver Creek Resort Company. I believe my successful navigation of this process was a direct result of the skills and techniques I applied from the book."
Tim Baker, Executive Director
Keystone Neighbourhood Company

"I can honestly say that *So, What's Your Point?* exceeded all expectations and will no doubt prove valuable in my professional and personal life. Thank you to the authors!"
Bryan Arnwine, Oncology Service Manager - Southeast
US Oncology

"This is probably one of the most practical books I have ever read. It made me realize that I have a great deal to learn about clear and concise communication."
Joel Schuh, Baylor Health Care System
Baylor Tom Landry Health and Wellness Center

"I am so excited to learn how to use these communication tools. Mind you, I had to consciously think through the models while I was conversing but when I used them, it was smooth flying! I want to thank you for an awesome tool. I have searched, researched, asked around for many years to find something that is easy to remember, fits in almost any communication situation yet works!"
Vicki Cain, Account Manager
Universal Weather and Aviation, Inc.

"Actually, in all honesty, I found this book most applicable to dealing with my teenagers. Our conversations are much more productive when I exhibit patience and really listen to them."

Bret Yeary, Project Manager
Xcel Energy

"This book truly inspired me and provided a plethora of tools that I can utilize to enhance my communication skills and ultimately my career."

Ryan Riddle, Accountant
Clayton Williams Energy Inc.

"I felt this book was incredibly beneficial and I am looking forward to continuing to develop and incorporate the lessons into my daily work activities."

Ryan Voorhies
BBVA Compass

"*So, What's Your Point?* has given me useful insight on how to phrase and construct sentences when I write or speak to other people in general, whether the topic is casual or professional. The information and skills I learned are invaluable and really do make a difference."

Chris McDonald
Baker Hughes

"Congratulations to the authors on an outstanding book. *So, What's Your Point?* is must reading for any dedicated professional who wants to be fully successful in his or her career."

Carl Wilson, Vice President & CIO
Georgia-Pacific LLC

"For years I've thought there must be some logical order to communicating effectively but could never put my finger on it. This book reveals the secrets to preparing, conducting, and analyzing effective communication in a logical, structured manner."

Kenneth T. Hertz, Administrator
M.D. Care, Inc.

"*So, What's Your Point?* is a standout! It hones in on the essential skills that are the core of all business relationships. It is a book you will turn to again and again."

Sandra J. Hale, President
Enterprise Management International

So, What's Your Point?

Fourth Edition

*Persuasively make your point,
increase credibility, overcome objections,
avoid misunderstandings and minimize arguments
in your professional and personal communications*

**A practical guide for learning and applying
effective interpersonal communication techniques**

James C. Wetherbe
&
Bond Wetherbe

Mead Publishing
Texas USA

So, What's Your Point?

Published by Mead Publishing
P.O. Box 6890
Lubbock, TX 79493-6890
U.S.A.
Phone: (713) 553-4020
       (281) 610-4064

ISBN: 978-1-883096-07-6

Mead Publishing books are available at special discounts for bulk purchases by corporations, institutions and other organizations.

For more information, please contact Mead Publishing at:

        Email: meadpublishing@att.net
        Website: http://www.meadpublications.com

Dedication

The best evidence of the value of good communication skills is our success in persuading our wonderful wives to share their lives with us.

To Brynn from Jim
and
To Faye from Bond

Acknowledgements

As we progress to the fourth edition of this book, we are grateful for the reviews, criticisms and recommendations offered by our many readers of previous editions and particularly for those who have spent time and effort reading the manuscript over and over to review the overall style, presentation and phrasing of the content.

Over the past 25 years we have been privileged to teach thousands of people in academia as well as in the corporate and professional world the interpersonal communication principles this book presents. Their show of appreciation and encouragement to continue to make this book available is both humbling and gratifying.

We also appreciate the efforts of our loved ones and family members who have internalized and practice the concepts presented in this book and continue to support us in our efforts to share these communication skills with others.

As we acknowledge the efforts of all who have contributed, we also assume full responsibility for any inadequacies or discrepancies in the text.

James C. Wetherbe   Bond Wetherbe

About the Authors

James C. Wetherbe

Dr. James Wetherbe is the Stevenson Chaired Professor in the Rawls College of Business at Texas Tech University. Author of 32 books, he is ranked among the top dozen consultants and speakers on the management of information technology and among the 20 most influential researchers in his field. Jim is internationally known as a dynamic and entertaining speaker who is especially appreciated for his ability to explain complex topics in straight-forward, practical terms that can be understood and applied by business leaders.

Mead Bond Wetherbe, Jr.

Bond Wetherbe is a professional faculty member in the Information Systems and Quantitative Sciences area in the Rawls College of Business at Texas Tech University. He was formerly the Director for the Center for Executive Development in the School of Business at the University of Houston where he managed the design, development and implementation of executive-level education programs and taught management and leadership courses at the undergraduate and graduate level. Along with being an educator, Bond is a business outcomes oriented consultant and author.

Table of Contents

PART ONE
Introduction

PART TWO
Verbal Communication Models

PART THREE
Non-Verbal Communication Skills

PART FOUR
Putting it All Together

PART FIVE
Expanding the Models

Preface

Perhaps the single most important skill a person can develop is the ability to communicate effectively with others. Only through effective interpersonal communication can one persuasively convey an idea, overcome objections, avoid misunderstandings, and minimize arguments.

Of the two major components of communicating—content and process—the process component overwhelmingly carries the stronger message. Developing and improving the process of both verbal and non-verbal communication through a step-by-step approach, focusing on basic fundamentals, is the theme of this book.

This book began as a seminar primarily aimed at helping computer professionals (who are generally regarded as less than excellent communicators) communicate more effectively. The concepts of the original seminar were by no means limited to technical people, and the demand for the seminar quickly expanded to other functional areas of business in every conceivable industry.

Invariably, when we conducted the training for developing and improving interpersonal communication skills, there were numerous requests for a book that explained the step-by-step approach used in the training process. Up until then, all we could provide was the training material and referral to individual notes taken during the training session. In completing the fourth edition, we are glad that we first presented the material in book form back in 1993.

Although this book is based on training material, anecdotes, and the experiences of both authors, most of it is written in the first person singular to give the reader a more personal sense of participation. Further, to distinguish between what someone is saying versus what someone is thinking, spoken words appear between double quotation marks while thoughts appear between single quotation marks. The authors' thoughts, i.e., *asides or parenthetical expressions,* appear between parentheses.

So, What's Your Point?

PART ONE

Introduction

*Eighty percent of the 'problems' in workplace or personal
relationships are really not problems—they are misunderstandings.*

1

Setting the Stage

Two friends of mine, Dick and John, were having a heated discussion about politics. Dick turned to John and exclaimed, "That's what's wrong with you bleeding heart liberals. Your giveaway programs to freeloaders cause hard-working people like me to be taxed to death!" John quickly retorted, "You cold-hearted capitalists are so self-centered and materialistic that you don't care about anybody but yourselves!"

I asked Dick, "Would you really want any American who truly wanted to work but was unable to find work have his or her family go without food or necessary medical care?" "Of course not!" Dick objected. "John," I asked, "Would you want any hard-working American to pay taxes to support people who would rather manipulate the welfare program than seek honest employment?" "Of course not!" John replied hastily.

"Are the two of you essentially agreeing with each other, but you just don't know it?" I teased.

This conversation between Dick and John typifies the polarization generally expressed between Republicans and Democrats in the United States. It is intriguing how quickly people adopt opposing positions when their basic attitudes are really not that different.

Guess what causes most of the problems in workplace or personal relationships? Eighty percent are really not problems—they are misunderstandings. What kind of commentary is that on our ability to communicate? Think about it—80 percent of the time there is not a problem; we are just not understanding each other.

The American Assembly of Collegiate Schools of Business (AACSB) did a survey of the most successful MBA graduates from the top ten business schools asking them to reflect upon their careers and to indicate the single most important skill leading to their success. Guess what the answer was? Interpersonal communication skills. Is it any wonder then that a good communicator can eliminate up to 80 percent of his or her "problems" by avoiding misunderstandings?

How often do you accomplish what you want to accomplish in an adversarial situation? Would you like to communicate so well you could avoid misunderstandings and concentrate on real problems? You can achieve that goal by mastering the techniques presented in this book.

The Case of the Mystery List

During a consulting project, a vice president of finance, Tom, sought my advice. Tom was about to fire Harry, his information systems director. "You know," Tom said, "it occurred to me that maybe I'm not assessing the situation correctly. I would really like an outside opinion of this person's abilities before I make my final decision."

In actuality, of course, he was probably looking for confirmation on his decision to dismiss Harry. Nevertheless, I agreed to talk with Harry.

In these situations, one of the things I like to assess is how a manager or executive views each of the people who report to him or her. When I say, "So tell me about the other people that report to you," and he or she responds, "Well, they're all jerks too!" I may get a clearer picture of the real problem.

In this case, however, Tom said the other three people who reported to him were very productive. The problem was just with Harry. "Can you do something for me?" I asked Tom. "What's that?" he replied. "Can you tell me the 10 most important things that you'd like Harry to do so you would be pleased with his performance?" I asked. "Sure," said Tom, "I can do that easily." As Tom itemized his wishes—a reasonable list—I jotted them on paper. We finished our discussion, and I left to go to Harry's office.

As I entered his office and introduced myself, Harry did not look particularly happy to see me. Yes, you guessed why—he viewed me as the hatchet man! Almost immediately he said, "Look, just tell Tom I'm looking for another job. I'll be out of here as soon as I find one. Just give me some breathing room." "Hold on a second," I said, reassuringly, "I'm just here to assess the situation. I'm not here to ask you to leave."

As we talked for a while, I perceived that Harry was a very dedicated, hard-working guy. In fact, he explained, "I've been putting in 60 to 70 hours per week. I work my butt off for Tom, but no matter what I do, no matter how hard I work, I just can't please him."

After a while I asked, "Harry, would you do something for me?" "What's that?" he responded. "Could you make out a list of the 10 most important things you think it takes to please your boss?" I queried. "Sure," said Harry, "I can do that."

He made his list, and I looked it over. It was also a reasonable list, but significantly different than Tom's. "You know Harry," I offered. "This is very unfortunate because I sense you're a hard-working, dedicated person who wouldn't deliberately perform badly. But I've got to tell you, I had your boss make a list of the 10 most important things he said it would take to please him. As I review your list, I'm afraid there's not much similarity to Tom's list."

At that point Harry did something very interesting. He scooted his chair closer to mine and probed, "You have a list of the 10 most important things it would take for me to please my boss?" "Yes," I replied, "I have it right here in my briefcase." Leaning a little closer, Harry offered (tongue in cheek, of course), "I'll give you $500 in unmarked bills at a discreet location in the parking lot at 5:45 p.m., if you will let me have that list!"

"Well Harry," I said. "I'd like to let you have it, but I'm just not sure it would be appropriate for me to just give you the information, considering the manner in which I gathered it. However, I do need to go to the men's room. If it's all right with you, I'd like to leave my briefcase here. I'll be back—let's synchronize our watches Harry —I'll be back in six and one-half minutes."

When I returned, the piece of paper with Tom's top 10 items was in my briefcase—still hot from the copy machine. We quickly finished our discussion, and I left.

Two months later, I received a phone call—Harry's boss, Tom. "You're incredible! I can't believe what you did for Harry. It happened right after you left. Everything I ever wanted him to do he started doing immediately. I've waited this long to call you because I thought it was a fluke, but after two months it is clearly a sustained change in behavior. It is nothing short of fantastic!"

"Well, that's great," I responded. "Did you get my invoice?" "Yeah, yeah!" he exclaimed, "but that's not what I wanted to talk to you about. Now that Harry is so good—you know those other managers who report to me ... well, they don't seem so good to me anymore. I'd like you to come back and do for them whatever you did for Harry."

"Look," I replied, somewhat apologetically, "I've got to be honest with you. I didn't do all that much." "What do you mean?" he exclaimed. "It's incredible! Harry is doing great!" "Look, Tom," I said, "Remember your list of the 10 most important things that Harry would have to do to make you happy?" "Yes...?" he replied. "Well," I said, "all I really did was arrange for Harry to get a look at the list."

There was utter silence on the phone—prolonged silence. Fortunately Tom's good sense of humor surfaced: "Well, that explains it!" "Explains what?" I responded. "The change in Harry," Tom chuckled, "He's been cheating!"

Unfortunately, we see this type of communication breakdown over and over again in simple, ordinary, everyday occurrences. How many times have you seen people in work or social situations vehemently complain about another person's behavior, but never provide sincere, constructive information to let him or her know there is a problem? Too often someone complains about someone else behind his or her back, leaving the offender in the dark, until the offended becomes exasperated and loses his or her temper.

The Case of the Missing Car

Let me share a personal example about the family automobiles. In the 1980s and 1990s I was a professor at the University of Minnesota in Minneapolis and also did a lot of consulting work in the business community. For business tax reasons, I owned three vehicles. One car was for my consulting activities, so I could take a 100 percent tax write-off without having to keep mileage records. The second was the family automobile—an SUV. And the third, was a little sports car which I drove back and forth to the University and for personal use. My wife and I had a two-fold agreement about the use of the vehicles: 1) the consulting car was not to be used for personal use because the 100 percent tax write-off might be invalidated; 2) the family car and the sports car were to be driven no more than 7,500 miles annually to comply with insurance discount provisions.

I returned from a three-day business trip, arriving on a Saturday, and the consulting car was not in the garage. When my wife returned later with the car I asked, "Why were you driving my car?" "Well, I'm getting too many miles on my car," she replied as she walked away. Her response did not make sense to me, since my car had more mileage than the SUV, but I really didn't spend time thinking about it as I was preoccupied with other matters.

Several days later, the same thing happened. When she returned I asked, "Why were you driving my car again?" To which she restated, "I told you, I'm getting too many miles on my car." "What are you talking about?" I questioned, "There are many more miles on my car than on yours." "I know that, but I'm talking about insurance miles," she explained.

As you have most likely discerned from these interchanges, this is a communication problem. Although we were both using the word miles, we meant something different, i.e., I meant total odometer miles, while she meant insurance miles. You see, her vehicle was getting too close to the insurance limit of 7,500 miles per year; so rather than change the insurance, she thought she would occasionally use the other car.

Given a choice and some time to think about the situation, my wife was actually taking the approach I would have desired she take. But when the conversations were occurring, I got irritated with her because it seemed to me that she was violating the agreed upon house rules. Thus, the problem was not with reality, it was with communication. Do you see how easy it is to misunderstand?

What I Mean Is What I Mean

We have many words and phrases that can be very misleading. Use of these words and phrases can lead to low-quality communication. Big problems or budget overrun can mean different things to different people. Have you ever been talking with someone and the other person comments, "Oh, that is going to be much too expensive!" or "That is going to take too long." Without really thinking you reply, "Well, we better not buy it then," or "We better not do it then." Sometime later you find out what the precise price or time requirement was and think, "That's not too high a price or time commitment."

This example highlights that in not knowing the exact numbers behind the generalizations *too expensive* or *too long*, we do not communicate effectively. Because individual perception is always a factor in any situation, we must try to be as clear and definitive as possible to have effective communication.

As a brief last example, I was in a restaurant when a vaguely familiar gentleman approached me, extended his hand, and said, "Hi, Jim. I'm not sure if you remember me—I know your wife better than you." Suddenly I realized that he meant, "I know your wife better than I know you," as I recalled that he and his family attended my church. Cordially, I responded, "Hello, Bill, it's good to see you." This conversation, as you can see, had the potential to lead to a major misunderstanding!

Philosophy of Good Communication

The philosophy for being a good communicator is very simple:

1. Assume 100 percent of the responsibility for understanding what the other person is saying and means.

2. Assume 100 percent of the responsibility for making sure that the person you are communicating with understands you.

If two people assume 100 percent responsibility for understanding and being understood, extremely effective communication occurs. Since most people do not take the time to make sure they are understood or that they understand, you usually have to cover for the other person to avoid misunderstandings. As we proceed through this book, we present the techniques to implement this 100% responsibility communication philosophy.

The point is that what seems natural or intuitive to you when learning a new skill is usually, and unfortunately, fundamentally incorrect.

2

It's All About Fundamentals

The key to mastering any communication or other skill, is understanding and internalizing the basics or the fundamentals. Have you ever participated in a sports activity—tennis, golf, snow or water skiing, softball, bowling, self-defense, etc.? How did you approach learning the sport? Did you, like most people, try the sport first and then later take lessons from a pro?

For those readers who took lessons from a professional, what did you find out about the techniques you used before taking lessons? Did you find you were doing most of the fundamentals incorrectly? Ninety percent of the time, people who start learning a sports activity on their own do things fundamentally wrong. (Do those of you who have not taken lessons for your sport of choice now realize how much they could help you?)

Knee-Jerk Reaction

The point is that what seems natural or intuitive to you when learning a new skill is usually and, unfortunately, fundamentally incorrect. One of the best books on golf says, "If you give someone a golf club and a ball and tell him to hit the ball, he will do everything fundamentally incorrect." The primary thing most people do fundamentally incorrect in a sport that involves hitting a ball, e.g., golf, baseball, tennis, squash, racquetball, is that they do not keep their eyes on the ball. They look where they want the ball to go instead of at the point of impact, and, as a result, often miss the ball.

This tendency is referred to as a *knee-jerk reaction*—one's *'automatic response'*. For example, if someone were to throw a punch at you, your knee-jerk reaction would be to flinch. If you take lessons in self-defense, you learn that flinching is an incorrect response—but it is an automatic or natural response. One of the key fundamentals in self-defense is to watch for what your opponent is going to do. For example, to defend or avoid an incoming fist you must watch it, step back, and with a sweeping arm motion, block the fist. If you close your eyes and turn your head, you will most certainly get hit.

Tennis Anyone?

Chances are, if I took you to a tennis court (assuming you have never played the game), gave you a tennis racket, and asked you to hit the ball back and forth over the net with me, this is what you would do naturally: (First, visualize that the ball is coming to your forehand side, i.e., the right or left side, depending with which hand you hold the racket). You would face the net, and as the ball approaches, you would have a tendency to continue facing the net as you hit the ball back over the net. Your knees are straight and you allow the ball to get too close and crowd your body. Just as you start to swing at the ball, you look up to see where the ball is going to go. All fundamentally incorrect!

What are you supposed to do? If you are right-handed, stand with your left shoulder facing the net, your left foot angled somewhat toward the net, your feet about shoulder-width apart, and your knees slightly bent. The ideal distance from the ball requires you to slightly reach for it. While keeping your eyes on the ball, step forward with your left foot pointing toward the net, and swing with your right arm as you rotate (snap) your hips toward the net.

When most people swing at something, they try to get their power from their arms. If you have taken lessons, you know the greatest power in a swing is produced from the large leg muscles as you snap into the swing—starting with your legs, rotating through your hips, and transferring to your shoulder and arm motion.

Of course, there are different fundamentals and visualization techniques for different types of strokes. For example, a right-handed woman executing a backhand stroke in tennis, she turns her right shoulder to the net and, while stepping forward and then rotating toward the net, pretending her racket is a sword, pulls the sword out of its scabbard and swings it in a sweeping motion toward the ball.

After Bill Cosby won the Celebrity Tennis Tournament several years ago, he was asked by an interviewer, "Last year you didn't play very well. How did you get so good in such a short time?" Cosby explained that he quit trying to play tennis his way. He took lessons, unlearned everything he was doing wrong, and learned the fundamentals.

Skiing the Rockies and the Lake

Snow skiing also provides an excellent example for analysis. Suppose I invite you to your first ski outing, strap two slick pieces of fiberglass on your feet, lure you onto a steep hill covered with snow, and instruct you to crouch slightly and lean forward or down-hill. Automatically, your brain's knee-jerk thought is, 'This does not seem right!' Next you find yourself wanting to stand up straight and lean backwards rather than crouching and leaning forward into the slope. And as you lean back, what happens? No control! As you start to slide, you gain speed, and leaning forward becomes even less desirable. So you lean back further. Well, now you can't turn—so you are going in a straight line downhill—fast! And, of course, you lean back even further as you prepare for impact!

Two key fundamentals you learn through ski lessons are to keep your weight on the balls of your feet, your shoulders and head facing downhill as you traverse the slope, rotating at the hips. To carve through the corners of the snow, you must have your weight forward—on the balls of your feet. If your weight is shifted back on your heels, you cannot execute a turn.

The knee-jerk reaction for water skiing is just the opposite: novice water skiers are going to land on their faces several times until they internalize the basic fundamental of exaggerating the backward lean. Water skiers have to learn to use their leg muscles to keep their upper body behind their feet. To get them to visualize or feel the correct position, instructors shout, "Try to drag your shoulder blades in the water!"

What Are Those Spots For?

Even the sport of bowling elicits an initial knee-jerk reaction in most people. When most people start bowling they aim at the pins. Where are you supposed to aim? At the spots painted in front of the foul line. They are much easier to see than the pins way down at the end of the alley.

Self-Defense—In Case You Can't Avoid Arguing

Earlier, I mentioned self-defense and the knee-jerk flinch when someone throws a punch at you. It is actually very easy to protect yourself if you know some fundamentals. For instance, someone can swing at you with the left hand or the right hand; or, someone can try to kick you with either the left foot or the right foot. Rarely does someone hit you with both hands or kick you with both feet at the same time! So, there is only one thing that can come at you at any given time.

In your mind's eye, visualize a panoramic view of your attacker. When the attacker comes at you with a right punch, it arrives from your left. The technique is to watch the punch, and as it starts coming, take a step away from it, and raise your left arm to block it. While the basic fundamental motions for blocking punches and kicks are easy, it takes training and practice to get yourself to stare down an incoming punch or kick and actually block it—overcoming the strong knee-jerk reaction to flinch or turn away.

So how do you learn the fundamentals? You take lessons, and then you **practice, practice, practice**.

*The best times to practice the techniques presented in this book
are in 'high stress, inconsequential' situations.*

3

Communicating Has Fundamentals Too

What is true about the fundamentals of sports activities discussed in Chapter 2 is also true about interpersonal communication skills, i.e., what comes naturally to us is fundamentally wrong. Again, some examples can quickly demonstrate the wrong and right ways to communicate.

When You *Screw Up*, Don't Hide the Screwdriver

Let's say you have *screwed up*. (Can you relate to that?) And now someone else is pointing out that you *screwed up*. What's your knee-jerk reaction? You get defensive, right? You try somehow to avoid getting blamed, to not look bad. However, if you really have *screwed up* and you try to blame someone else or won't admit the mistake, does that make you look better or worse? Once again our knee-jerk reaction is fundamentally incorrect.

While it doesn't come naturally, the best thing you can do if you've really *screwed up* is to admit it. Suppose someone says, "You know, you really *screwed up* on that one; you should have gotten it right the first time." Your reply should be, "You're absolutely right. What I did was wrong and I feel awful about it." What can the other person say in response? (Most likely your response has ruined the other person's day!) The other person was ready to beat you up about it and now he or she does not have the opportunity. The correct approach is that no matter what is said, you absorb the assault and admit you are wrong. It immediately takes the wind out of the attacker's sails.

Conversely, when you won't admit to a mistake you've made, most people just won't let you forget it. I happen to believe that Richard Nixon's presidency could have survived Watergate if he had said, up front, that it was a mistake and assumed full responsibility. In fact, Barry Goldwater made the same observation. As long as the media and the public felt Nixon was not *fessing up*, they wouldn't let Watergate rest.

No Need to Argue Anymore

Through reading this book, you have the opportunity to learn some very different and very powerful communication techniques. If you master these techniques, I propose that you will not get into any more arguments—unless you choose to. Arguments are absolutely dysfunctional—because nobody really wins an argument. If you lose, you lose. And if you win the argument, you still lose because that other person is going to be waiting to get even. The next time that person catches you in a position where you can be *nailed*, he or she is going to get even. So, you never really win arguments in the long run. The point is, you don't want people waiting to get even with you.

Please don't misunderstand. I am not saying that I don't get into arguments. In fact, I can be very hot tempered. But I use the techniques in this book for important professional and family matters, so I have not had a professional or career-related argument in over 25 years.

There are two times when I inventory all of my hostility, and then let it all come out. The first is when I get outrageously bad service. The second is when someone is rude on the highway. Not too long ago, a guy literally looked me right in the eye and ran me off the road. I caught up to him at the next traffic light, got out of my car, and broke off his antenna. It felt so gooood! It still feels good when I think about it! Now, I'm not proud of that childish behavior, I just want to point out that all of us lose our tempers from time to time and throw technique out the window. Since that episode, my family calls me the antenna terminator.

Don't Practice on Your Boss

In the chapters to come, we present exciting and powerful communication techniques. One of the questions that frequently comes up when we teach these techniques is, "How and where do I practice this stuff?" Well, for starters, don't try these techniques on your boss tomorrow! The best times to practice the techniques presented in this book are in high-stress, inconsequential situations. And what are those situations?

The Antenna Terminator Behaves Himself

Let me share an example of how I have practiced the techniques.

I was exiting a parking lot and had to cross two lanes of oncoming traffic, but I couldn't get across because the traffic was so heavy. (I'm convinced there was someone down on each end of the block with a stopwatch staging cars—Go! Now! Now! Now!—just to make sure I could never leave.) So I sat there, and I waited and waited, and finally I saw the best gap I thought I was going to get. I pulled across the two lanes, and as I merged into traffic, an orange Dodge Ram Charger ran right up to my rear bumper. I could see its big grill, sneering at me in my rear view mirror. Then it swerved around and back in front of me, barely missing the front of my car—with the driver sharing his IQ with me, using a familiar hand gesture.

My defensive nature was immediately triggered. I had been waiting in the parking lot for what seemed like 15 minutes. I had to get home for dinner—what was I supposed to do, pack a lunch? And now I had to deal with this guy sharing his IQ with me. As my middle finger started throbbing in knee-jerk response, I tried hard to gain some control and thought to myself, "Well, this would be a good time to practice my interpersonal skills—this is a high-stress, inconsequential situation!"

Practice on the Road

So I followed the guy to the intersection, pulled up behind him and waited for the green light. There appeared to be a woman in the car, and I assumed the driver was saying non-complimentary things to her about my driving. I saw him checking me out in his rear view mirror, while I just sat back there sedately in my sedan. Then it occurred to him that I might be giving him obscene hand gestures from the outside of my car, so he checked his side mirror.

I sat there with both hands on the wheel thinking, "OK, just calm down, stick to the fundamentals!" That's when I decided to follow him—wherever he went. He turned left, I turned left. He turned right, I turned right. He changed lanes, so did I. All of a sudden he developed a newfound interest in me, so he speeded up. I sped up. I was right with him; no gestures, just driving along.

Finally, he pulled into a parking lot, which was apparently where he lived, and jumped out of the Ram Charger. He had apparently given instructions to his passenger (who turned out to be his teen-age daughter), and she was making a beeline toward the apart-ment complex. He approached me as I got out of my car, took a John Wayne stance, and said, "What's the matter with you? When you pulled in front of me like that, I could have smashed right into the back of you! Are you crazy?"

Looking him straight in the eye, I said, "You're absolutely right. The minute I saw you in my rear-view mirror I realized I had made a mistake. I followed you to apologize. I am so sorry."

Have you ever seen someone suck air? His daughter even slowed down and looked back. "Now who looks bad?" I thought. "I didn't realize how fast you were coming," I added. "How fast was I going?" he questioned, like he expected me to declare, "Too fast!" Instead I stated coolly, "I don't know, but it doesn't matter. It was my responsibility to judge how fast you were going because I was the one who was merging, and I misjudged completely." After stut-tering for a moment he replied, "Well, that's something we all do at one time or another." "Well, I just wanted to let you know I'm sorry," I tendered again, as I climbed back in my car and left him on cordial terms.

Graduating to Consequential Situations

If you recall, I prefaced the above example by suggesting that these interpersonal skills are best practiced initially in high-stress, but inconsequential situations. I was not trying to establish a relationship with the driver of the car in the above example, I was just practicing my interpersonal skills. Receiving bad service at a hotel, restaurant, or retail establishment provides an excellent opportunity to practice overcoming knee-jerk behavior. Remember: high stress, low risk are the practice watch-words. As you gain skill and confidence in the techniques covered in this book, you can begin to apply them to high-stress, high-risk situations—with your boss, customers, management, spouse, or significant other.

Sixteen and Shy

Let's look at some other situations where our knee-jerk reactions are fundamentally incorrect. Consider social situations.

When I was 16 years old, I had to transfer to a different high school for a year because my mother had to relocate to attend graduate school in another state. When I started at the new high school, it was very difficult for me to make friends. When you are 16, you do not walk up to a group of kids and say, "Hello, I'm the new kid..." I responded to the situation very normally by letting shyness take over and withdrawing from situations rather than getting involved—the infamous Fear of Rejection controlling my behavior.

After some time, I got to know a few classmates—and guess what they revealed, "We thought you were really stuck up." So my knee-jerk reaction of shyness was perceived by my peers as aloofness and arrogance.

There are some very straightforward techniques for dealing with that particular situation, and they are presented later in the book. Right now, we are concentrating on knee-jerk reactions and undesirable outcomes. I wanted to be friendly and make friends, but my knee-jerk response had the opposite result.

The Helpful Jerk

Suppose you are standing alone, holding up the wall at a social gathering where you know no one. Suddenly a group of people gather in front of you and start talking about something in which you have enormous expertise—traveling abroad. As you listen, one person says things that are incorrect. What's your knee-jerk reaction? Correct him, right? You think to yourself, "Hey, I better get right in there!" Quickly, you put on your commando parachute and come to the rescue! "Excuse me," you blurt, "I happen to have traveled in Europe extensively and what you're saying is not quite correct. What happens is ...."

What's your objective? To make a positive impression? To have people exclaim, "Wow—what a genius"? Instead they think, "What a jerk!"—especially the person that you corrected. Again, the knee-jerk reaction is fundamentally incorrect.

My Movie Please

Consider the issue of control. Suppose you and your significant other are trying to decide what movie to see. Your companion says, "How about a romantic musical?" "I don't want to see that fluffy stuff," you reply. "I was thinking of an action thriller." "I don't want to see that stupid stuff!" says your companion.

I suspect we can jointly write the remainder of this script: "We went and saw what you wanted to last time," you respond. "Yes, but two times before that we saw your movie," declares the companion. "Yes, but if you recall, last summer...."

And so it continues until we have enough recalls to develop a frequency distribution on who made the decision regarding every movie we have seen since the beginning of the relationship—with the objective of out-tabulating the other person, because the one who tallies the most points wins. But remember there is never a winner in an argument.

Suppose I win and we go to the movie I choose. What will my companion do? She will probably say something like: "Are you enjoying this?" "Did you know it was this bad?" "You probably did not know it was this bad, did you?" "Did you even bother to read the reviews before you selected this?" And, of course, I would feel obligated to provide the exact same *courtesy* should I have been out-tabulated and had to attend my companion's movie.

Now let's reconsider the objective: to have a pleasant evening. From my perspective, the ideal scenario is to go to my movie and have my companion enjoy it. The second best option is to go to my companion's movie, have it turn out to be really interesting, and thoroughly enjoy it. Because of our knee-jerk behavior, however, neither of these ideal scenarios are likely. Instead we are relegated to these alternatives: 1) I get to go to my movie, and my companion ruins it for me; or 2) we go to my companion's movie and I ruin it. Has either person won?

Our knee-jerk reaction when others do not let us do what we want to do is to try to force them. While it's not our natural response, here's the best response for the movie scenario: "The most important thing to me is for us to have a good time together, so let's go see your movie." If you say that, you have a 50-50 chance of getting to see your movie. Again we can write the script from there. My companion will likely respond, "Aaww no, let's go see your movie." "No, no, no, we should go see your's this time..."

Mirror, Mirror

There is an interesting effect called mirroring that happens in relationships. In mirroring, people tend to do what you do. So, if I'm being selfish toward you, you tend to act selfish toward me. If I'm being generous you tend to be generous.

Let me give you an example. Suppose that we go to lunch together. Afterwards, the waiter brings the check to the table. I reach for the check. What is your knee-jerk reaction? You reach for the check too, right? But let's say I pick up the check this time.

When we have lunch again two weeks later, you will likely insist on paying for the check. If the check were brought to the table and I tried to pick it up again, we would most likely get into a tug of war over the check because you would be insisting, "Let me, it's my turn." The mirroring effect is controlling our behavior. You're willing to argue to pay for the check.

Suppose, however, after the waiter set the check on the table I said, "You know, I did pay for lunch the last time, so it's really your turn this time." (What would you want to do with that check?!) Even though it is your turn, and even though you are willing to pay for it, when I say, "It's your turn," you actually wish that you could say (at a minimum), "Now wait a minute. If you remember, I picked up the check two times in a row before the last time we had lunch together." It's the mirroring effect. Selfishness begets selfishness; the unpleasant begets the unpleasant. Generosity begets generosity.

When we discuss body language later in the book, you will discover that people actually emulate your non-verbal messages. If someone really feels comfortable with you, he or she will frequently assume the same standing or sitting position you have taken. People mirror each other's body language if they are feeling good about what is happening.

Jealousy, the Ultimate Turnoff

Let's consider jealousy—the ultimate dysfunctional behavior. I am referring to real jealousy, not the kind you use to flatter someone. What is our natural response when we get jealous? We tend to get hostile, right? Our objective is to hold on to what we have.

Suppose you want to play golf on the weekend and your spouse says, "Why do you always want to play golf? Why don't you spend more time with me?" Does that inspire you to spend more time with that person? (Now, I'm not a golfer, and having played golf a few times, I personally think it is a sure way to ruin an otherwise pleasant walk in the woods. And, I am convinced that a lot of people play golf just to get away from someone who is saying, "Why don't you want to spend more time with me?")

Jealousy can actually make a person do exactly the opposite of what you want him or her to do. It is a knee-jerk reaction that drives people away. If someone wants to play golf or go ice fishing (There's an interesting pastime! I've always thought it must take a really poor relationship to force someone to sit on ice in sub-zero temperatures, jiggling a fishing pole), the most effective response is to say, "I hope you have a great time. I'll look forward to your company when you return."

Jealousy at the High School Reunion

Imagine you are attending the high school class reunion of your significant other. At the high school reunion some *bozo* or *bozette* is really paying a lot of attention to your significant other. Afterward, as you're driving home, you confront your partner with, "So who was the bozo hanging all over you?" Offhandedly your partner replies, "Oh, that was Tom, a guy I dated in high school." "You dated that guy in high school? You have got to be kidding! What did you see in him? I hear he spent some time in the penitentiary!"

Again—what's your objective? To try to make yourself look better than your spouse's old flame. Have you accomplished that?

The much more difficult, and much more effective behavior is to be complimentary. "Who was that guy paying so much attention to you?" you ask with interest. To your spouse's response, "That was Tom, a guy I dated," you counter with "Well, he seemed like an interesting guy. I enjoyed talking with him and can see why you dated him," (as you chew off the inside of your cheek).

If you express jealousy in a flattering way, such as, "I hate to admit this, but I was feeling a bit jealous watching the two of you recall old times," you are in control and your jealously may not even have been perceived by your spouse. However, when it becomes a divisive or ridiculing form of jealousy, it can be very dysfunctional. We are never less attractive than when consumed by vile, hateful jealousy—not effective behavior for competing with whatever or whomever caused the feeling of jealousy.

Master the Fundamentals

These examples demonstrate that what we tend to do naturally works against us. To overcome our knee-jerk reactions, we need to learn some fundamental skills. Do you want to play tennis well? Learn the fundamentals of each stroke: the serve, forehand, backhand, overhead, etc., and then put them all together to play the game well.

Do you want to have good interpersonal skills? Master the fundamentals.

Content deals with <u>what</u> you are communicating.
Process deals with <u>how</u> you are communicating.

4

Content versus Process

In the next few chapters, we are going to be focusing on the fundamentals of effective communication and learning some very simple, useful, verbal communication models. But first, there are two very important aspects of communicating we must consider:

1. **Content**
2. **Process**

Content deals with **what** you are communicating. **Process** deals with **how** you are communicating. It is important to know that **process preempts content**.

For example, if you ask me a question, the way I answer your question can make a significant difference in our relationship. One way I can answer is, "Hmm, that's an interesting question," and then give a thoughtful and considered response. Another way I can answer your question is to sneer at you. Without saying a word, I convey the attitude of 'How could you ask such a stupid question?' followed by a short, curt answer. At that point, how I answered— my condescending manner—becomes more important than whether or not I answered your question. The **process** overwhelmed the **content**.

When two people argue, it is generally because of **process**, not **content**. They are not treating each other with respect or consideration. And, it does not matter what the **content** is, the issue becomes how they are treating each other—the **process**.

The Good Samaritan

I was driving along the highway on my way home one winter night when I noticed a car alongside the road with the hood up. An elderly man and woman were standing beside the car. Since it was cold and snowing, I thought they might appreciate some help. So I stopped my car and started walking back to them. They peered at me as I approached them and asked, "Hi there, are you having car trouble?"

From a content standpoint, that is a ludicrous question. What are they going to say? "No, no trouble at all, our motor enjoys fresh snow whenever it gets a chance." Of course not. The man replied, "Yes, although I'm not sure what the problem is. Would you be willing to give us a ride to the service station down the road so we can see about getting a tow?" By asking a question that had an obvious answer, I was really demonstrating that I was friendly and wanted to be helpful without alarming them regarding my intentions. It was the process that mattered.

All Content and No Process Equals
All Work and No Play

One of the managers in a company with which I am quite familiar used to take his in-basket to meetings with his peers or staff members. Whenever the meeting shifted to casual conversation or shooting the breeze, he started doing paperwork. Occasionally, he looked up and checked the conversation. When it shifted back to work-related issues, he stopped doing his paperwork and participated in the meeting. When someone brought up the subject of weekend activities, he delved back into his paperwork.

It probably would not surprise you to learn that until he changed this behavior, he was never really included in the management team. He viewed the meetings as a functional activity as opposed to a process. He did not realize that communicating with others in the meeting established rapport—asking questions about things people are interested in is integral to process.

Model Your Communication

Let's consider some basic models that isolate the communication process. When you're communicating, you can actually categorize the interaction into six basic processes. Referring back to our analogy of playing tennis, when someone communicates, he or she sends something over the communication net. Responding might require the equivalent of a forehand stroke or a backhand stroke; it might require a lob; or it might require an overhead slam. And of course, sometimes you serve. To become a tennis player, you have to master the backhand, forehand, lob, slam, and serve. The same holds true in the sport of communication.

The verbal communication process can be categorized into six different models (communication strokes):

1. Explanation
2. Agreement
3. Closure
4. Reservation/Doubt
5. Question/Confusion/Conflict
6. Query

To become a good communicator—effectively deal with what comes over the communication net—you must master the fundamentals related to these six models. In the following chapters, we discuss each of the six models in a very straightforward manner —using examples to illustrate how each model works and how they all work together. The fundamentals for learning each model are as simple as learning how to keep your eyes on the ball or step into a swing.

If you have ever taken any lessons for a sports activity, you recall that the fundamentals were generally easy to explain, e.g., keep your eye on the ball; however, they required drill and practice to master. So it is with learning how to communicate effectively. When you have finished this book, you will have learned what you need to know to communicate effectively and how to drill and practice to perfect and master these skills.

So, on to the first model ... **Explanation.**

PART TWO

Verbal Communication Models

*If you could observe yourself, you would be surprised at how often
you assume other people know what you know or can read your mind.*

5

Explanation Model

The Explanation Model is used to communicate an idea, a concept, a request, or a proposal. An explanation has two parts and they are sequential:

1. Problem
2. Solution

Most people offer the solution without explaining the problem —the knee-jerk reaction. For example, I approach my boss and say, "Well, we need John to work overtime this weekend." That is a solution. To John it is a problem—it is inconvenient for him. It is also a problem for my boss—it impacts the budget. My boss may have to provide justification to his boss. What is good about John working overtime? Nothing!

Here is another variation on the solution without an explanation conversation between me and my boss:

"I need John to work overtime this weekend," I state.

"I don't want John to do that. It's not in the budget," my boss replies.

"Well, we'd better do something, because if John doesn't work overtime this weekend, 10,000 people won't get their paychecks on Monday."

Is John going to work overtime this weekend? You bet he is!

Let's take a look at what I just did from a process perspective. In this case, my boss took a position: John was not going to work overtime this weekend. And, what did I do? I forced him to reverse his position.

Do you like taking a position in a conversation and then being forced to change it immediately? What if someone else is standing there watching as it happens? Imagine your boss is in the room and a subordinate comes in and asks you a question. You answer, "No." Then the subordinate gives you some additional information, and you respond, "Oh, well, in that case the answer is yes!" How do you feel about having to change your position?

Say So in the First Place

Let's return to the conversation about John working overtime. If, late in the conversation, I add information, my boss is likely to reply, "Well, why didn't you say so in the first place?" That is exactly the underlying logic in this model: say so in the first place. State the problem before offering a solution.

Using the correct approach, I could improve the communication as follows: "The payroll transactions came in late today, and there is not enough time to get them processed so people can get paid on Monday. John is available to work overtime this weekend to complete the processing. May I have your approval?" Do you see the difference?

The Basic Model for Commercials

This basic problem/solution model is used in approximately 80 percent of all the TV commercials. The following examples of commercials illustrate the construct of this basic model:

> **Problem a:** "Ring around the collar"
> **Solution a:** "WashOut, the latest detergent"
>
> **Problem b:** A little leaguer slides into second base with white pants on and gets a grass stain
> **Solution b:** The kid walks in the door and his mother cries, "Oh, Steve, get the StainOut!"

Problem c: Billy Bob is at a square dance and complains to Randy, "Betty Lou won't dance with me for nothin'."

Solution c: Randy pulls him off to the side and says, "Billy Bob, it's your breath. It smells like a gallopin' buffalo! You need to use this 'Breath Fresh' toothpaste." Five minutes later, Billy Bob is on the dance floor with Betty Lou.

Are you beginning to see how this model works? When used for mass communication it seems rather trite. However, the explanation model is basically what you see in all commercials, and it is based on sound psychological principles. The idea is to reach out with a hook to relate you to a common problem. You think about Billy Bob trying to get Betty Lou to dance with him, and you start reflecting, "You know, I haven't been that socially successful myself lately. Maybe ..."

Linked by Association

The other type of approach is what's called the associative commercial. The associative commercial links something or someone with a product. For example, a commercial shows a star basketball player leaping high off the court to retrieve a rebound, with the camera focusing on the Nike basketball shoes he is wearing. Next we see him running down the court and flying high above the rim to slam dunk the ball in the basket. Again we see the Nike shoes and the screen fades to the Nike motto, *Just do it*! The obvious goal is to get you to associate high performance athletic ability with wearing Nike shoes. Advertisers display something uplifting and then the product to create the association in their viewers' minds.

In another commercial you see people having fun and laughing, then you see beer—associative commercial format. Alternately you see people in the middle of the desert with a beer truck, and you think "dry and thirsty." The next second, everyone is having a great time and nobody is thirsty—problem-solution format.

While associative commercials are used frequently, problem-solution advertisements are much more common. The problem-solution format is a psychologically sound way to communicate an idea, concept, or proposal.

Programmed for Misunderstanding

Stating a solution before explaining the problem can cause enormous misunderstandings, as illustrated by the following example. When I lived in Minneapolis I was conducting a seminar for a local company. During a break, I used the telephone in the room to call a music store to check on some equipment I had ordered (I didn't have my cell phone with me). I did not know the telephone number for the music store, so I looked around for a phone book. There was no phone book, so I tried to call information. The phone was programmed so it could not access information. So I called my home, but no one was there. Realizing that I was running short of time, I called my secretary. Let me assure you before I continue, she's a wonderful person.

"Hello, Kathy?"

"Yes?"

"Could you look up the phone number for the NewSound music store for me?"

What do you think her perception was? "He is too lazy or too cheap to pay 50 cents to call information!"

Kathy looked up the number and relayed it to me—with a definite strain in her voice.

After she hung up the phone, I suddenly realized what I had just done. So I called her right back and said; "Kathy, what did you think when I asked you to find that phone number?"

"Do you want me to tell you the truth?"

"Yes, I do."

"You're very presumptuous."

"I am really sorry. Here is what happened. I am at an office phone and ... ," I explained. Kathy laughed and replied, "It's OK, I understand."

Had I not called her back and explained the situation, it would not have been unreasonable for Kathy to assume I was too lazy or too cheap to look up the number myself.

Let's examine what might have happened had I not called her back. After giving me the phone number for the music store and hanging up, Kathy turns to Judy, another secretary in the office, and shaking her head exclaims, "I don't believe this!"

"You don't believe what?"

"Wetherbe"

"What did he want?"

"He just called to have me look up a number for him in the yellow pages."

"You looked up a number for him in the yellow pages?"

"Yeah!"

"Are you telling me that he called you to have you look up a number in the yellow pages for him?"

"Yeah!"

"Wow!"

Judy leaves the room, walks down the hall, and says to the next person she sees, "You are not going to believe what Wetherbe does every time he wants something looked up in the yellow pages. He calls Kathy and asks her to look it up. I'll bet he calls her at home on the weekends!"

What an opportunity for rumors to get started. Fortunately that didn't happen since I called Kathy back and explained my situation. Again, let people know what the problem is so they can better understand the solution. I should have explained my predicament before asking Kathy to look up the phone number.

Three Problem/Solution Guidelines

Here are some guidelines for using the explanation model:

1. Complete the explanation of the problem before you discuss the solution.

Wrong: "The payroll transactions came in late, so we need John to work overtime this weekend. Otherwise, people won't get paid on time."

The solution is sandwiched within the problem. At the point in time that you start asking your boss for something, he or she has most likely filtered out anything else you're saying and is trying to think of objections.

Right: "The payroll transactions came in late today, and there is not enough time to get them processed so people can get paid on Monday. **[problem]** John is available to work overtime this weekend to com plete the processing. Is that OK with you?" **[solution]**

You want to make sure your boss really understands the problem and is convinced it needs to be solved.

2. Make sure there is a logical progression of thought to the explanation.

Ask yourself, "In what sequence or order should I present the information related to the problem and solution so the listener can easily follow what I'm saying?"

Here's a good example. I was driving to a shopping center with my wife. As we came to an intersection, I asked her, "Is it clear to the right?"

"Yes..., as soon as this bus passes," she said. As soon as I heard "yes", I stepped on the accelerator. By the time she finished the sentence I was halfway into the intersection, desperately trying to get the car into reverse to avoid being hit!

A response that follows a logical progression of thought would have been, "After this bus passes, go for it antenna terminator!"

Returning to our basic example:

Wrong: "I'm afraid that people are not going to get their pay checks on Monday. There is not enough time to get them processed. They came in late."

Right: "The payroll transactions came in late today. There is not enough time to get them processed in order to get people paid on Monday." And, go on from there.

3. When stating a problem, include an impact statement.

Wrong: "The payroll transactions came in late. Can John work overtime this weekend?"

You are assuming that your boss realizes the impact of the payroll transaction arriving late. That can be a mistake. Remember, you take responsibility for making sure that your boss understands the cause and effect relationships of the problem. So be sure you state the impact resulting from the problem.

Right: "The payroll transactions came in late today. As a result, there is not enough time to get them processed today in order to get people paid on Monday. Is it all right with you if John works over time this weekend to ensure that people get their paychecks on Monday?"

Read My Mind

If you could observe yourself, you would be surprised at how often you assume other people know what you know or can read your mind. For example, you might approach your boss and say, "Do you mind if I take off early this afternoon?" To your boss, all you've said is that you would like to take off early this afternoon. Your boss may be thinking, "I really need you here this afternoon, I wonder why you want off early. If it's to play golf then the answer is no. Should I ask? I really don't want to be nosey. However, if I don't think it's a good reason ..."

Rather than put your boss in that situation, why not say, "I've had a severe toothache since this morning. I called my dentist and she can fit me in at 2:30 this afternoon. Do you mind if I take off early to make that appointment?"

Or, you may have a situation where out-of-town guests are arriving for the weekend. "I'm having some family visitors this weekend. Their flight arrives at 3:00 p.m. and I would like to be at the airport to meet them when they arrive. Is it all right with you if I leave work early this afternoon in order to meet their flight?" Again, the point is to explain the problem before offering a solution.

Skill Drill

The secret to learning and internalizing these communication skills is drill and practice. Take a few moments and construct an explanation. Write it on a piece of paper. It can be work related or non-work related. Choose something that is related to a problem or situation you are currently facing: perhaps a misunderstanding with a neighbor; a problem between you and your significant other; a situation at work with your boss, a co-worker, or a subordinate. Just take a moment. Keep it very short. Construct a one or two sentence problem, followed by a solution statement. Writing it out like a script in a play may help in preparing to present it. In fact, you should be able to read it right to the person to whom it is directed.

Review your explanation and check for the following:

1. Is your explanation of interest or concern to the listener?
2. Does your explanation follow a logical progression of thought?
3. Have you included an impact statement in your problem section of the explanation?
4. Have you completely expressed the problem before offering the solution?

Chapter 15 includes some tips and techniques on how to practice with the models. As you continue through each chapter, refer to your written explanation and continue to build the script as you learn each new model to provide a starting point for developing your practice drills.

If possible, practice (role play) your explanation with a friend. Find out if he or she feels that you have developed your explanation according to the above guidelines. Don't worry about dealing with any responses just yet. We will discuss responses in the following chapters.

Explanation Model Summary

Do you feel like you have a basic understanding of the explanation model? If not, reread this chapter. Remember our objective is to avoid knee-jerk reactions that can lead to misunderstandings, so: 1) break the communication process down into specific identifiable parts; and, 2) analyze and understand those segments.

Just like one must learn and practice the various tennis strokes to master the game of tennis, one must study and practice these communication models to master the art of effective interpersonal communication. When you complete an explanation, for example, the person listening can potentially respond to you in a variety of ways. Oh happy day if the response is in agreement with what you just said! And that leads us into the next model... **Agreement.**

As simple as this Agreement Model is, providing reinforcement and expanding is not a knee-jerk reaction.

6

Agreement Model

During the course of an explanation of a problem and solution, you may experience agreement on the part of your listener. When agreement occurs, you have an opportunity to use the Agreement Model, which consists of two steps:

1. **Reinforce**
2. **Expand**

Reinforce

Reinforcement occurs through the use of reinforcing phrases such as: "You're absolutely right;" "Good point!"; "Right on!"; or, "You've got it." These phrases make the listener feel good and think positively about what you are saying. As a listener, when you comment in agreement with someone who is explaining something to you and he or she says, "You are right about that!" it makes you feel good. You understand the situation and have contributed to the conversation.

The 'I' Syndrome

There is a danger, however, of a knee-jerk reaction when reinforcing your listener's agreement comment. That knee-jerk reaction is in the use of the first person pronoun, 'I'. For example, we easily say:

"I think that would be a good idea."
"I think you are right."
"I agree!"
"I know!"

While you are to be commended for using the first rule of the Agreement Model, reinforcement, you may be offending your listener by interjecting '**I**'. Or, at the very least, you would be negating the impact of reinforcing your listener's agreement by switching the emphasis back to you through the use of '**I**'.

Here is an interesting little game you can play. When you are talking on the telephone, create a scoreboard. Every time the person you are talking with says the word '**I**', give him or her a point. Every time he or she says "you," give yourself a point. Guess who is going to get the highest score 90 percent of the time?

When you hear someone say, "One of the things I like most about the alternatives I have presented is that I can achieve my goal by ...," how do you react? Positively or negatively? If, instead, you feel included in a conversation, how do you react? When someone says your name or uses the pronoun you, it triggers you — it energizes you, doesn't it? To include your listener, use the other person's name and the pronouns, "you" or "your."

When someone makes a comment of agreement and I respond with, "I agree," it implies that I approve. However, if I respond with, "That is a good point, Ted!" it implies that I'm impressed. And I have elevated him in terms of the conversation. So when you have the opportunity to reinforce someone, avoid the knee-jerk reaction of saying, "I know" or "I concur," and focus on the other person by saying, "**You**'re right!" or "Good point!" (implying "**You**'ve made a good point.").

Expand

After you have reinforced the agreement, you advance to the second stage of the Agreement Model and expand on the agreement. Let's go back to our example of the payroll transactions arriving late. You approach your boss and say, "The payroll transactions came in late today. There's not enough time to process them so people can get their paychecks on Monday. Is it OK if I ask John to work overtime this weekend in order to process the transactions?"

"We must get people their paychecks!" responds your boss.

Since your boss has responded positively (indicating agreement), you might say, "You're absolutely right!" [to **reinforce**]. If people don't get their checks, we will never be forgiven," [to **expand**].

Do you see how the Agreement Model works? First you **reinforce**, then you **expand**.

Agreement Before Solution

Occasionally a person may agree that the problem you have presented is indeed a problem before you have a chance to propose the solution. Again using the basic example, you explain to your boss, "The payroll transactions came in late today and there is not enough time to process them to get people their paychecks on Monday."

"Oh no, we have to get people their paychecks on time!"

Notice that you have not yet presented the solution. However, you can reinforce and expand by saying, "You're absolutely right. If people don't get their checks, we will never be forgiven. What would you think about having John work overtime this weekend to complete the transaction processing?"

"Well, John is the most qualified person." (You have agreement again.)

"That's true, he's handled it on several occasions in the past."

Now you and your boss are interacting positively—"you're on a roll" using the Agreement Model effectively.

Reinforcing and Expanding Is Not Knee-Jerk

As simple as this Agreement Model is, providing reinforcement and expanding is not a knee-jerk reaction. At least one of the reasons why we do not naturally reinforce and expand is because we are too self-centered. When people make supportive comments to us, we have a tendency to ignore what they have said and continue talking.

Some time ago, I conducted the Interpersonal Skills Seminar that this book is based on for the Executive Development Center at the University of Minnesota. After I finished the seminar, one of the students, Joe, approached me and said, "This interpersonal skills training has just been wonderful. It is really going to be useful to me, and I want you to know I put in a good word for you with your boss, Ken."

Ken was the program coordinator, a colleague from another department—not my boss. Well, I got caught up in that technicality, and this was my knee-jerk response: "Actually, Ken is not my boss. He is a colleague in another department." "Oh, sorry, I was just trying to help," Joe replied as he sheepishly backed away with an embarrassed look on his face.

What happened? I punished someone for being supportive. What should I have said? "Thank you very much, that was very thoughtful of you, Joe." To avoid an awkward situation for Joe at some future point, I could clarify that Ken is not my boss. Otherwise, I could ignore the assumption Joe made.

Because of my self-centeredness, I reacted badly—the knee-jerk reaction. I didn't want people thinking Ken was my boss.

Here is another response I could have used: "Thank you very much. Ken and I have been working together for some time on Executive Development Center programs, and although Ken is not my boss, thank you for your kind remarks."

Agreeing to Disagree

One of my favorite examples of people not listening for agreement or supportive remarks occurred on television right after President Reagan had been elected for the second time. Senator Robert Dole was a guest on the *Nightline* program along with Professor Milton Friedman, the well-known Nobel Prize-winning economist from the University of Chicago.

Ted Koppel, the *Nightline* host several years ago, turned to Professor Friedman and asked, "What do you think about the state of the economy now that we've gone on to Reagan's second term?" Friedman replied, "Well, I think that overall the economy is much better off than it was four years ago. Inflation is down and unemployment is down. Things look pretty promising for the future. There is one fundamental problem that has to be addressed, and that is the national deficit. The only way that will be resolved is if legislation is passed that requires a balanced budget because there is too much pressure put on the legislators by special interest groups for them to ever solve the budget problem unless they're mandated to do it by law."

Senator Dole, Republican and house minority leader, responded something like this: "Well, all I have to say is that it is real fine for those of you in academia to talk about what is wrong or needs to be done. The rest of us, however, have to deal with the real world."

What was he doing in his response? Since he assumed Milton Friedman was going to slam dunk him, Dole planned to discredit him for being an academic, regardless of what he said. Obviously, Dole was not listening. Friedman, an independent, Nobel Prize-winning economist, painted a very favorable view of the Republican administration and endorsed the exact legislation Reagan wanted passed. Instead of seizing the moment, agreeing through reinforcement and then expanding on Friedman's comments, Dole responded in the all too common knee-jerk reaction mode.

Dole, like we have all done at times, was so certain that Friedman was going to disagree with him that he made no allowance for agreement. Someone may try to change his or her position and come around to our viewpoint, but we won't let them because we are being defensive. We are set for an argument and are not really listening to what the other person is trying to say.

Agreeing When You Don't Mean To

You may find yourself using the agreement model when you don't really agree. For example, suppose someone says something you disagree with, but the statement is factually correct. In response you reply, "Well, that's true," usually followed by "but,..." or you may say, "Good point, but..." In your mind, you are acknowledging the statement's accuracy, but you are not agreeing with the person's viewpoint. In his mind, however, he thinks that since you acknowledged that he is correct in what he said, you must have agreed with him.

Have you ever had something like that happen? In several of the following chapters, we discuss situations in which someone doesn't believe you or disagrees with you, and we present techniques to prevent that type of misunderstanding from happening.

Agreement Model Summary

Remember, when you are having a discussion with someone, or giving an explanation, look for agreement or listen for supportive statements, then reinforce and expand before continuing. The Agreement Model should be used when someone agrees with your problem and/or your solution.

If the conversation has come to an end and you have had nothing but agreement, then you are ready to move to the next step of the communication process... **Closure.**

*Now that you have finished everything you want to talk about,
it is time for a close.*

7

Closure Model

The **Closure Model** allows you to focus upon and quickly review the results of a conversation. The process is simple and straight-forward. Imagine you have completed a conversation in which you have had agreement with a proposed solution. Now it is time to wrap up the conversation and be on your way. The two steps of the Closure Model are:

1. **Review Points of Agreement**
2. **Propose Course of Action**

Using the Closure Model

The first thing to do in closing is to **review the key points of agreement**. There are always at least two: 1) the problem and 2) the solution generated from an Explanation Model. However, you may have had a conversation in which you've discussed several things. So you simply review all the things you've talked about. The second part of the Closure Model is to **propose a course of action** for either you or the person to whom you have been speaking.

Let's apply the Closure Model, again using our example from previous chapters:

"The payroll transactions came in late today and there is not enough time to process them to get people their paychecks on Monday." **[problem]**

"Oh no, we have got to get people their paychecks on time."

"You are absolutely right." **[reinforce]** They would never forgive us if we were late getting their checks delivered. **[expand]**. Would you approve overtime if I ask John to work during the weekend to get the checks processed?" **[solution]**

"Well, John is the most qualified person."

"That's true.**[reinforce]** He has handled payroll processing on several occasions in the past." **[expand]**

"OK, go ahead and schedule John to work overtime this weekend."

At this point, you have agreement on both the problem and the solution. You may want to continue the conversation by saying, "You know, this payroll problem is starting to be recurrent. This is the fourth time in the past seven weeks that the payroll department has been late with the transactions." **[problem]**

"Four times in seven weeks, that's outrageous!"

"You're absolutely right. **[reinforce]** Every time they do this it puts us at risk and causes budget problems. **[expand]** What would you think about getting together with Donna in payroll the beginning of next week to discuss this problem?" **[solution]**

"Fine, make it first thing Monday morning."

Is that supportive? Absolutely, so you reply, "Good point! **[reinforce]** The sooner the better." **[expand]**

A Time to Close

Now that you have finished discussing everything you wanted to talk about, it is time for a close. You say, "All right, the payroll transactions came in late and we want to make sure people get their paychecks. John is available to get the transactions processed over the weekend, so I will schedule John to work overtime this weekend. We want to avoid this problem in the future **[points of agreement]**, so I will set up a meeting with Donna at 8:00 a.m. on Monday." **[propose course of action]**

48

Leaders of meetings generally review points of discussion and action items at the end of meetings. When you've been meeting for an hour or more, it is very helpful to review the key points and then propose a course of action. While it may seem a bit unnecessary to conduct a review for our short example, it is part of assuming full responsibility for effective and accurate communication.

No Surprise in the Close, Please

During a close avoid introducing an issue that has not been discussed previously. New items can cause confusion and clutter up an otherwise clean closure. For example, it would be a bad idea to include in the preceding closure example, "and since overtime is no problem as far as the budget is concerned..." This was not a point of discussion and it might open up other issues to deal with in an otherwise clean close, which leads to the next model...
Reservation/Doubt.

*Reacting to someone having reservations or doubts
about what you are saying by going directly to
substantiation comes across as a counter-punch.*

8

Reservation/Doubt Model

All of the prior model discussions have been examples of *sweetness and harmony*. Realistically, we know that conversations have many characteristics, and a variety of things can happen during a conversation. For instance, the person you are conversing with may not believe you. What might he not believe? He may not believe that your problem is really a problem. Or, he may not believe that your solution will work.

Again (using the basic example) you go to your boss and say, "The payroll transactions came in late today and there is not enough time to get them processed so people can get paid on Monday. Is it OK to have John work overtime this weekend?" Your boss may reply, "Wait a minute, I'm not at all convinced that overtime is called for. Can't you just get people to hustle between now and 5:00 p.m., and get the transactions processed on time?" In this case, your boss doesn't believe the problem is really a problem.

Or, your boss might say, "Wait, I am not convinced that John has enough experience to handle something as important as getting the payroll transactions processed." In this case, your boss doesn't believe your solution will work.

Don't Slam Dunk

As it turns out, the more you may be in the right, i.e., what you're saying is true, the more likely you are to cause a **process** problem. Why? Because in your mind, you have things under control, and you just can't believe your *stupid* boss is giving you static about your assessment of the situation. You just want to *slam dunk* him.

At this point, one of the things you need to be aware of is that the other person is generally thinking more about himself or herself than about you. You may tend to think that he or she is questioning your judgment or even calling you a liar by expressing doubt or disbelief at what you have just said. When your boss says, "Wait a minute, I am not at all convinced overtime is necessary...," you tense up and become defensive. Instead, it is important for you to understand your boss's perspective. Contrary to what you think at the time, he doesn't think you are a liar; he just doesn't want to have to pay overtime unless it's absolutely necessary. If he doesn't believe that your assessment is true, he is not going to go along with your solution. If he does believe your assessment, he has to agree to paying overtime. Therefore, his knee-jerk reaction may be that believing you is not in his best interest. Do you understand what's happening here? He is thinking about his concerns, not yours.

Just Because You're Right, Don't Start a Fight

Again, the more you are in the right; the more likely you are to cause a process problem. For instance, your boss says, "Wait a minute, I'm not at all convinced that overtime is necessary. Can't you just get people to hustle up a bit between now and 5:00 p.m., and get the transactions processed on time?" You reply, "Are you kidding, we are talking about 14 hours worth of work! Generally, that's two full-time people working all day to get it done. We've only got one hour left today with just two people in the department. How do you expect ...?" What you really convey with that response is anger with your boss for not believing what you are saying and questioning your decision. The defensive posture and associated anger are not good technique!

Don't Get Angry, Communicate

In a situation such as this you need to use the **Reservation/ Doubt Model**, where you:

1. **Reassure**
2. **Substantiate**

This model does not come naturally. The knee-jerk reaction is to go directly to substantiation, which involves providing evidence to support the issue being doubted. Reacting to someone having reservations or doubt about what you are saying by going directly to substantiation comes across as a counter-punch. Someone takes a jab at you, then you give a jab right back.

Here is how reassurance works: let the other person know you share his or her values. In our example, you only want John to work overtime if it's really necessary. And, that's exactly what you need to convey to your boss. He says, "Wait a minute, I'm not at all convinced overtime is necessary. Can't you just get people to hustle up a bit...?" You should reply, "Well, we certainly don't want to have someone work overtime unless it is absolutely necessary." Would your boss agree with that statement? Of course he would. Psychologically, you have taken him from a doubting frame of mind to an agreeing frame of mind. You have reassured him that you have the same concerns that he has about using overtime unnecessarily.

Follow that reassurance with a **substantiating** statement such as, "Here's what we are up against. We have 14 hours worth of work to get done, which we normally do with two people in one day. There is only one hour left in the normal work day and two people who can do the work. We could ask some of the other employees to help, but they aren't really very familiar with the processing and would most likely just get in the way. There is just no way we can get the processing done in an hour. We really are facing an overtime situation."

No Need to Argue

Notice that there is nothing argumentative about what you are saying, "Here's what we are up against...." You are explaining the situation. The message comes across as, "We are both reasonable people. Neither one of us wants to ask someone to work overtime unless it's really necessary, but this is why it's necessary."

What if your boss says, "I'm not sure that John has the experience to handle that by himself." What's the reassurance? You should reply, "Certainly we want to make sure that whoever we assign can get the job done." You let him know that you share the same concern. The real issue, however, is whether his concern is valid. The reassurance phrase acts as a buffer between his reservation and your substantiation in order to make your substantiation less confrontational.

After giving your boss reassurance, you can follow with, "The reason I suggested John is because he has single-handedly processed these transactions on four or five previous occasions—twice on overtime and at least twice when they came in a day early. We can be comfortable with his experience level." You have avoided process problems that can lead to an argument. With this approach you have substantiated your explanation without being argumentative.

Reassuring Is Not About Agreeing With the Doubt

There is a very important subtlety to understand about reassurance. In the above example during the reassurance step, you are not indicating whether John is competent, but rather that whoever is assigned has to be competent to get the job done. Similarly, on the overtime issue during the reassurance step, you are not indicating whether overtime is necessary, but rather that overtime should not be used unless it's necessary. These are non-argumentative statements.

The key to effectively dealing with someone who expresses reservation or doubt about your problem or solution is to avoid the knee-jerk reaction of becoming defensive and immediately sub-stantiating your position. Consider the other person's perspective, then offer **reassurance** that he or she can agree with before pro-viding non-argumentative **substantiation**.

Other responses that you might encounter call for a different strategy, which leads to the next model...

Questions/Confusion/Conflict.

For quality control reasons, you should rephrase every time to achieve your goal of being an excellent communicator.

9

Question/Confusion/Conflict Model

Other than someone agreeing with or doubting your explanation, you may be faced with a question about your explanation, confusion about the situation, or conflict from the person with whom you are communicating. The key is to recognize which communication ball is coming over the net so you can prepare the proper return stroke. The **Question/Confusion/Conflict Model** consists of:

1. **Rephrase**
2. **Answer/Clarify/Minimize**

The Continuing Saga of the Late Payroll

After you have presented your explanation, your boss may have a **question** such as, "Hasn't John put in an awful lot of overtime lately?" Or, even though it is not true, your boss may be **confused** and say something like, "Forget it, John has put in too much overtime already!" If John has worked a lot of overtime already (i.e., the boss is not confused), genuine **conflict** exists. Note that your boss may say the same thing for confusion or conflict. The difference between the two is the accuracy of the boss' statement.

Here are other examples of conflict (if the following are true): 1) "Absolutely not, we don't have the money in the budget for the overtime!"; 2) "No way! Prior written approval is required from top management for overtime, and it is too late to get approval now!"

Whether you are dealing with a question, confusion, or conflict, the first step is always to rephrase. For example, your boss says, "Forget it, John has put in too much overtime already!" A rephrase is simply, "You're concerned about the amount of overtime John has worked?" Or, if the boss says, "We can't do it; we don't have the money in the budget!" you rephrase, "Oh, so you're concerned about the budget?" he says, "No way, there is not enough time to get top management approval in writing," you rephrase with, "So, your concern is making sure we have prior written approval for overtime from top management?"

Why Rephrase?

The importance of rephrasing is based upon the philosophy for being a good communicator: *assume 100 percent of the responsibility for understanding someone else, and assume 100 percent of the responsibility of making sure that someone else understands you.* If there is one time that it is important to understand correctly what someone is *saying* and what someone *means*, it is when they are starting to get upset—a conflict situation. You rephrase for four important reasons:

1. To validate the communication;
2. To create an agreeable mind set;
3. To force yourself to listen; and
4. To allow you more time to formulate an answer.

Each reason is discussed below.

Did You Mean What You Said and Did I Hear It Right

The first reason for rephrasing is to *validate the communication*. Rephrasing is something you do spontaneously when, in reply to someone's statement or comment, you say: "Let me see if I have this right. You are saying ..." Take a moment and think about when you have done that. Has it been when you thought you understood something, but you were not sure? When you were quite certain that you understood something the first time, you likely didn't confirm it with a rephrase did you?

The problem is that it is possible to be fairly certain that you've understood something when you have not. In fact, there is a good chance that some aspect of the communication was lost. The person speaking to you has a thought in his or her head and converts that thought into words. Can something deteriorate in that process?

Then, the words float through the air to your ears. Can something go wrong? Your concentration may be distracted by some noise or visual interference. After the words impact your ears, you have to convert them into your own thoughts. Anywhere during the communication process there can be a problem.

When you are uncertain whether you've heard some statement correctly, you'll automatically say, "Did I hear you correctly?" For quality control reasons, you should rephrase every time to achieve your goal of being an excellent communicator. By the way, when you do this, approximately 50 percent of the time the person you're talking with responds with additional words of clarification or qualifies by saying, "That's not exactly what I mean. This issue is more about..." Or you may have completely missed the boat and he or she will say, "No, that's not what I mean at all." Whether you think you've understood or not, rephrase to be sure. It is worth it.

From Negative to Positive Before We Continue

The second reason to rephrase is to *create an agreeable mind set.* Your boss states, "Forget it, John puts in too much overtime already!" You reply, "Oh, so you are concerned about the amount of overtime that John is working?" How do you think your boss will respond? Positively, right? By getting your boss to say "yes" you change his or her mindset from a negative, disagreeable frame of mind to a positive, agreeable frame of mind. When your boss "begins nodding" in a positive frame of mind, he or she is more receptive to the next idea you present than if he or she is in a negative frame of mind.

Have you ever seen two people arguing with each other, and, as an observer, it appeared to you that they were really in agreement with each other but they just didn't know it? (Remember Dick and John discussing politics early in Chapter 1?) In this situation, one person is thinking 'no' to everything the other one is saying. That is why it is important to get the other person to respond positively. You want to change the person's frame of mind. You do that by rephrasing what the person said and asking for confirmation. If the person does not say, "Yes," and alters what he or she said or what you thought he or she said, you rephrase again, continuing to do so until you fine tune the point of disagreement and obtain agreement with your rephrase. (My record for this is five rephrases.)

You Cannot Rephrase What You Did Not Hear

The third reason the rephrase is so important is to *force yourself to listen*. There is only one way that you can successfully rephrase what someone has just said, and that is by having listened to what was said in the first place. So the rephrase forces you to listen when it is probably the most difficult time to listen. When someone is being disagreeable, you begin to panic. You begin getting *hot under the collar* and ready to either make your point more forcefully or become defensive. The technique is to think to yourself, 'Okay, this looks like a conflict situation and I have a discipline for handling conflict. When I recognize it, I just step back and listen to what's being said. I don't think about anything else until I understand and can successfully rephrase what has been said.'

Take Some Time; You Probably Need It!

The fourth reason for rephrasing is to *allow you more time to give an answer*. Don't rush yourself. Our knee-jerk reaction when someone disagrees with us is to interrupt the other person before he or she finishes disagreeing. We want to stop the disagreement.

Professor Jekyll and Professor Hyde

Let's go through a role-playing exercise to illustrate the impact of listening and giving a thoughtful response. Pretend we are in a university classroom situation and you are one of 30 students in the class. As the professor, I've been discussing two concepts, A and B. (Notice, we are talking process not content here.) During the lecture, you raise your hand and say, "Wait a minute, aren't you contradicting yourself when you say A and B?" I curtly respond, " Not at all! In fact, if you check your reading assignment from last week, the issues are covered in quite a bit of detail on pages 22 and 23. Any other questions?"

What did I just do? *Slam dunked* you, right? How do you feel about me right now? Any negative vibes? How do you think the rest of the class feels, especially if any one of them has some comments or thoughts they would like clarified? They don't want to be treated the way I just treated you, so they will more than likely not say anything.

Now, let's consider another response to your comment about contradicting myself. I pause, look toward the ceiling as though I'm searching for an answer, and politely say, "So, you feel that A and B are contradictory concepts?" You reply, "That's right!" Then, after a short pause, I say, "Let's take a look on pages 22 and 23, where the issues are discussed. Let's see if this clarifies your concern about them being contradictory." And, then I explain why A and B are not contradictory.

Do you perceive the differences between the two processes? Did I slam dunk you? What are you thinking now? As you gaze around the classroom with a smug look on your face, you think to yourself, 'See how he had to struggle to answer my question? Did you see him ponder? I don't ask light-weight questions, folks.' Do you like it when you ask a question and the person who is considered an expert has to think it through before answering? Although it's my job to give an answer, does the way I answered your question the second time make others more willing to ask questions?

One of the worst things that can happen when communicating is that people won't tell you what they don't like about your ideas. If you become defensive or argumentative when people have questions or offer critique, then they stop giving you feedback and just offer passive resistance in other ways, and you won't get a chance to deal with it.

Does it make me look bad to not have a quick, snappy, pat answer? Not at all. A quick answer can make a question seem trivial. Instead, if I take time to think about what I want to say, I convey that the question was thoughtworthy.

Remember, time is yours to take. You come across better and are more appreciated for taking the time to consider and give a thoughtful answer.

Rephrase Review

Here is a quick review of the four reasons why the rephrase is important when dealing with a question, confusion, or conflict:

1. To validate the communication;
2. To create an agreeable mind set;
3. To force yourself to listen; and,
4. To allow you more time to formulate an answer.

When discussing the rephrase process during the seminar on interpersonal communication skills, participants occasionally object to rephrasing. For example, someone might say, "This rephrasing issue concerns me. Won't people get irritated when you repeat what they say?" To which I respond, "So you are concerned about sounding like a parrot?" "Exactly!" the other person replies, without noticing that I just rephrased their objection. This always gets a good laugh in the class and makes the point that rephrasing does not mean repeating.

There is an art to rephrasing effectively. One can paraphrase, as in the example above, or use the discovery rephrase (i.e., "Oh!, I see..."). Another approach is to be contemplative (i.e., "Hmmm... so you are really saying..."). The rephrase should not sound like a mechanical recording. To avoid that, practice using the different styles of rephrasing until they become comfortable additions to your set of communication skills.

Think of rephrasing as a quality control tool. Effective use of the rephrase can lead you to the real issues that are of concern. For example, your boss may initially object to John working overtime because of an *insufficient budget*. Then, as a result of your rephrases, he switches to another objection, *lack of lead time for approval*, before he eventually tells you, "My annual performance bonus is based in part on minimizing overtime expenses." Now you know where he is really coming from, and you can communicate more effectively.

The Question Is...?

If you are dealing with a question, the second step (after the rephrase) is to simply **answer** it. If your boss says, "Wait, hasn't John put in a lot of overtime lately?" you rephrase, "You would like to know how much overtime John has been working?"

"Yes, that's right."

"John's record indicates that he hasn't worked overtime in several weeks. I confirmed that with him and he said he is available to work this weekend."

See how it works?

However, the conversation may go something like this:

"Wait, hasn't John put in a lot of overtime lately?"

"So you want to know the amount of overtime John has been working?"

"Yes, that's right."

"John has worked overtime four times in the past six weeks."

"I thought so. I think that is excessive and unfair to John."

Now you are dealing with a situation where a question has escalated into conflict. So you rephrase with, "You think it is unfair to ask John to work overtime this weekend?" (Then, switch to the model that deals with conflict, discussed later in this chapter.) Remember, the rephrase should always be done in the spirit of wanting to better understand, never in an angry tone.

To Eliminate Confusion, You Clarify

Instead of a question, you may be dealing with confusion. If so, then you need to clarify. For example:

"Forget it! John has put in a lot of overtime lately."

"So you're concerned about the amount of overtime John has been working?"

"Yes, that's right."

"I could be wrong and I will be happy to check, but I don't think John has worked overtime for several weeks." (This is the one time when you should use 'I' instead of 'you'. By saying, "I could be wrong ...," you avoid conflict and create a mirroring effect.)

As discussed in Chapter 3, there is an interesting phenomenon that occurs when interacting with people. They tend to reflect the way you treat them. If you are kind and considerate, they are too. However, if your behavior is stubborn and bull-headed, others behave the same way, because people tend to mirror the way others treat them. By telling your boss that you could be wrong, it makes it comfortable for him to say, "Well, please check on that. I could be wrong, and if so, go ahead with your plans."

If your boss says, "Forget it! John has put in a lot of overtime lately!" (however, you know for a fact that he has not) and you reply, "No, he hasn't!" might you be heading for conflict? (Again, the more you are in the right the more apt you are to cause a process problem.) Your boss may well react to your statement with, "Well, I think he has!" In response you say, "Look, I've checked, and I know I'm right!" Now your boss is really irritated. You both can't be right. So, your boss may simply say, "Forget it! John is not working overtime this weekend and that's final!"

Have you ever had THAT happen? And then you walk away, shaking your head and thinking, "Boy, that's stupid. I told him that John hasn't been working overtime but he denied my request for no apparent reason." Actually, the reason is very apparent when you think about it: your boss doesn't like to lose arguments and can declare victory arbitrarily whenever he or she feels like it! And that is what just happened. Your boss decided to show you who wins arguments, demonstrating that process takes precedence over content. You see, it is an issue of process. Your boss can simply pull rank on you. That is the reason why you want to avoid allowing confusion to escalate into an argument.

Don't Argue, Minimize

What do you do when you are facing a situation where there is genuine conflict? You want to **minimize** it. This is the case where John has in fact worked too much overtime, or there is no money left in the budget for overtime, or approval in advance of working overtime is required. How do you resolve conflict by minimizing? You present the *yin* and the *yang*. The basic philosophy is that there is a good side (yin) and a bad side (yang) to everything. When applied to a situation, whether or not I should do something is based on the good *outweighing* or *offsetting* the bad. A raised objection becomes the bad part of the idea. The trick is to not argue that the bad isn't bad, but that the good more than offsets the bad.

Minimize With Alternatives

Suppose you are facing an appendectomy. Your knee-jerk reaction before the doctor explains the procedure and results, is "Oh, gosh, I just don't want to go through surgery. I'll have a terrible scar." You may react that way because the word "scar" by itself is an example of low-quality communication. (Do you remember our discussion from Chapter 1?) If the word 'scar' were mentioned to a group of people, each one of them would most likely have a different picture in his or her mind of what it meant. Some may visualize a scar they actually have. Others may think of Frankenstein's scars, resembling giant centipedes.

Therefore, pretending I'm the doctor, I should say, "So, you're concerned about the scar?" After a response of "Yes", I should continue with "Let's talk about what it would look like. The surgery requires about a six-inch incision that, when healed, leaves a thin line that is barely detectable."

"Oh, I was thinking it would look like a big puffy centipede. What you are saying doesn't sound bad at all."

After that, quickly go to the Agreement Model.

However, let's say that you respond with, "I don't care. Any kind of scar looks bad and I don't think that I'll look good in my bikini."

"So, you're concerned about how you'll look in your swim suit?"

"Right!"

"You are just overreacting. The scar is not going to be *that* bad." (Notice that I (the doctor) have begun *arguing* with the patient — a frequent communication mistake.)

"That's easy for you to say. You're not the one who has to live with the scar!"

Am I going to win the argument over whether a scar is good or bad? No way! What should I be arguing? The alternative! For example, "So, you're really saying that any type of scar is distressing to you?"

"Yes!"

"Well, even though it is unpleasant, we must consider the alternative to not having the operation and the resulting scar—you could die!"

Does that put things in perspective? Pointing out *offsetting* advantages is how you minimize.

Returning to our basic example, your boss says, "Forget it, the funds allocated for overtime have already been spent!" You rephrase, "So, you are concerned that there is no money left in the overtime account."

"That's right."

You minimize, "Well, it looks like we are facing the greater of two evils. We have to ask ourselves, what is more upsetting to upper management: 1) a $250 overrun in the overtime account; or, 2) 10,000 people complaining because they did not get their paychecks on Monday?" (That puts it into perspective.)

For any objection raised, you point out the offsetting issues that minimize the objection. If your advantages don't offset the disadvantages, then you don't have a strong case. Make certain you present your case in the best possible way by considering the trade-offs.

Minimize Through Compromise

Another way to minimize is through compromise. If there is no funding available for overtime, you could suggest that John be given double compensatory time off next week to make up for working during the weekend. That's an example of a compromise approach to minimize a conflict.

Model Responses

The key to using each of the models effectively is to learn to recognize responses. Learn to look **for agreement; reservation or doubt; questions, confusion, or conflict** — then respond accordingly.

One of the most frustrating things that can happen during communication is to receive a negative, content-free response. For example, when using the Explanation Model, you ask if John can work overtime this weekend, and your boss replies, "No, I don't think so." You are faced with a response with no content. He just said, "No", without any reason why. A rephrase at this point is useless: "So you are saying 'No'," you state. He responds, "Yes!" and you have a conversation that is not progressing. What you need is some content. The next chapter presents the method for obtaining content through the use of the most important communication model... the **Query.**

Without a doubt, the question is the single most powerful communication tool you can learn.

10

Query Model

The final verbal communication model, the **Query Model,** is also the most effective. (We saved the best for last.) The Query Model is based on the use of:

1. **Indirect Probes**
2. **Direct Probes**

Without a doubt, the question is the single most powerful communication tool you can learn, as discussed later in this chapter. But first, let's examine how the Query Model works.

The Easiest Query

As discussed in the previous chapter, the key to mastering the communication process is learning to recognize and categorize responses and to apply the appropriate model. When you encounter a conversation where no content is offered in the response, use the Query Model to probe for content to further the communication.

When your boss says, "No, I don't think so," without giving any reason why, do an **indirect probe**. (This is the easiest one.) You simply say, "Oh?" What does "Oh?" convey? It is a solicitation for more information. Your boss may then reply, "There is not enough money in the budget for overtime." Now, you have some information to use!

Still No Content?

What if you query with "Oh?" to obtain some content and your boss replies, "No, I just don't want John working overtime this weekend." Still no content, right? Do another indirect probe such as, "Could you help me understand why?" or you could say, "Any particular reason?" or "Could you share the reason with me?". Usually your boss will give you a reason.

Categorizing Content and Responding

When the person with whom you are communicating provides content, you need to categorize it and respond accordingly. Your boss may reply, "I just don't think John has enough experience to handle payroll processing by himself." Use the **Reservation / Doubt Model** and provide reassurance that someone without adequate experience should not be handling the job, followed by substantiation that John is indeed qualified to process the payroll by himself.

What if your boss responds with "No way!" to your request for John to work overtime. You probe indirectly with "Oh?" He declares, "Absolutely not!" You probe again, "Could you tell me why?" And he says, "I just don't want to do it." You do not want to go to a third indirect probe because then you become a pest. Another indirect probe may provoke him to raise his voice and say, "Listen, didn't you hear me? I said 'NO', now get out of here!"

Direct and Subtle

Rather than probing indirectly for the third time, do a subtle transition into **direct probing**. An indirect probe is a content-free probe. When you say, "Oh?" you are not adding any content. A direct probe on the other hand does have content. For example, you could ask, "Does it have anything to do with the budget?" He may reply, "No, it's not the budget." Then you ask, "Anything to do with John's abilities?" He replies, "No, that's not it. What's irritating me is that the payroll department keeps getting these transactions in late and we keep covering for them and..." Now you have some content with which to proceed!

Puppy-Dog Eyes

If you haven't obtained any content after a few direct probes (i.e., you can't think of any more), switch back to an indirect probe such as, "I'm sorry, I'm just not understanding (sounding very apologetic). Can you help me understand what the problem is?" Usually your boss will give you an explanation if you probe correctly.

The primary thing to avoid is sounding like a cross-examining attorney. You must not give any indication that you are threatening or becoming argumentative. An effective technique is to use *puppy-dog eyes*. When you probe, do it with a sincere effort of wanting to know why, and raise your eyebrows with a wide-eyed expression that conveys, "Please help me understand." We discuss *puppy-dog eyes* and other non-verbal messages in greater detail in Part Three.

Remember, you are using the probe to obtain content when initial responses are negative but not specific. Ninety-nine percent of the time you will get content, information you would not otherwise have obtained, if you diplomatically alternate indirect probes and direct probes, and do it with *puppy-dog eyes*. Acquiring information is what enables you to develop win-win situations.

Under No Circumstances Will I Give You Content

Asking for information and conveying that you would like to understand the other person's point of view rarely creates a communication problem. Nevertheless, in every interpersonal skills development seminar at least one of the participants raises the issue of the *impossible* person who wants to be difficult no matter what happens.

The best way to demonstrate how to deal with such a situation is to conduct a role-playing session with the participant playing the role of the *impossible* person (a role he or she generally relishes). The objective is to demonstrate through use of the Query Model how to guide the obstinate person into a situation that clearly reveals he or she is being ridiculous without saying so directly.

An actual role-playing session from a seminar serves as an effective illustration. A participant in a class wanted an example of how to avoid creating a problem in a situation where content was being withheld, i.e., when you ask a question to obtain essential information and receive a response such as, "You don't need to know that".

Here is the situation: A project status meeting regarding the progress of the design and development of a new computer-based credit application processing system is just concluding. As people are leaving the room, the technical team leader from the Information Systems Department approaches and starts a discussion with the credit supervisor from the Finance and Accounting Department who has been assigned project management responsibilities.

(Note: I'm playing the role of the technical team leader and the student is playing the role of the totally uncooperative credit supervisor.)

Team Leader: One of the critical pieces of information we need to develop the new system is the criteria for how the credit decisions are made. Without that information, we can't develop the decision-table that determines how we process credit applications. [**problem**] Would it be possible for you to share that **information with us?** [**solution**—Explanation Model]

72

Credit Supervisor: I don't think you need to know that.

Team Leader: Oh? [**indirect probe**]

Credit Supervisor: Yeah, it's not an issue relevant to developing the system.

Team Leader: So you're saying that you don't think we need to know the criteria for credit decisions to develop the system? [**rephrase— Question/Confusion/Conflict Model**]

Credit Supervisor: Exactly.

Team Leader: Well, when credit applications are processed on the new system, the credit decision is a function of the software. My team is responsible for putting that computer code into the system. [**clarify—Question/ Confusion/Conflict Model**] How do we do that without knowing the credit **decision criteria?** [**direct probe—Query Model**]

Credit Supervisor: Look, I'm the boss here.

Team Leader: Absolutely [**reinforce**], that's why your input on this is so important. [**expand—Agreement Model**] You see, at the point in the credit application process where the software determines whether or not to grant credit [**problem**], the code has to be based on your decision. What would you like the code to do at that point? [**solution—Explanation Model**]

Credit Supervisor: It doesn't matter (the role-playing student is really reaching at this point).

Team Leader: Oh? [**indirect probe—Query Model**]

Credit Supervisor: Look, it doesn't matter what the criteria are at this point.

Team Leader: So what you're saying is that it doesn't matter what the computer program does about credit decisions? [**rephrase—Question/ Confusion/Conflict Model**]

Credit Supervisor: Right! At this point, I just don't care.

Team Leader: Are you saying that it's all right for us to go ahead and make the decision using criteria that we develop? Please help me understand what you are saying. [**rephrase— Question/Confusion/Conflict Model**]

Credit Supervisor: I'm saying I don't want to deal with that issue right now.

Team Leader: So, if you don't want to share the credit criteria information, whose criteria do you want us to use when we write the code? [**direct probe—Query Model**]

At this point, the participant playing the role of the credit supervisor generally says something like, "I see what you mean. Continuing to be *impossible* when someone uses query techniques with the Communication Models makes things very awkward and difficult. You feel like you are in a checkmate situation."

When it's obvious that information is being withheld, you need to use the Socratic Method of questioning. That is, ask questions that make the listener think and realize that he is being unreasonable, leading him to the necessary conclusion. You are able to make your point without ever telling the other person that he is being unreasonable or ridiculous.

Be Sure to Keep Your Cool

When dealing with difficult people, be sure not to lose your cool by telling the other person that he or she is being a jerk. Just keep asking questions in a helpful and constructive manner. Don't question the other person's authority or intelligence. Phrase your questions in a tone and manner of wanting to help and/or understand.

If you encounter a situation where you are dealing with a dominant, insecure type who feels threatened by your skillful use of queries, and he or she says something like, "I don't care, just get out of my office!", the best approach at that time may be to leave. (If that person is your boss, definitely get out of there! There is always another day and a better mood.)

Here's the point. Just as taking tennis lessons to learn the fundamental strokes required to play the game enables you to win more games, there may be situations where you simply cannot overcome your opponent. Learning and practicing the communication fundamentals presented in this book enables you to have more successful conversations than you normally would because you create more win-win situations. Through using the communication models, you can avoid arguments and accomplish what you want to much more often than you are now.

Fortunately, Most People Are Reasonable

Remember, most people are reasonable and respond positively to effective communication. Of course, there are always a few exceptions, and you have to work around those people.

Generally, I have found that when a person acted like a jerk, it was because I angered or insulted him or her and didn't even know it until later. Unfortunately we can become so caught up in what we are after that we don't even think about how others are going to react.

Do you recall the *Programmed for Misunderstanding* section in Chapter 5, when my secretary thought I was a jerk because I called and asked her to look up a phone number for me. I was so caught up in what I was after, being pressed for time and needing to get back to class, that I wasn't thinking of her feelings or how she might perceive my actions.

Query Before the Big Game

As mentioned earlier, the Query Model can be used to acquire more information when you get a response that's not rich in content. Above and beyond that, the question is the single most powerful tool in your communication arsenal.

To illustrate, let's fabricate a ridiculous conversation. Let's pretend that I am the head football coach for Texas Tech University and we, the Red Raiders, are about to play our arch rival the University of Texas Longhorns. I telephone the Longhorns coach and say, "You know, there is a lot of pressure on us to win this game, it is important to my career and future contract. My coaching staff and I were trying to figure out if we should go with an offensive strategy of a running game or a passing game. It occurred to me that you know your defense much better than we do. What do you think?"

The Texas Longhorns coach replies, "I'd go with the passing game."

"Now, when you say passing game, do you mean short or long passes?"

"Go with the short passes."

"Why?"

"Because you'll never have time to get off a long pass."

"OK, thanks. What about our running game? Should we try and run outside or up the middle?"

"I wouldn't try up the middle."

"Oh, so you know about our interior offensive line, huh? So tell me, from how far out can your field goal kicker put one through?"

"Oh, I'd say he's good for 35 to 40 yards out."

"Would you be willing to commit that you would not try a field goal outside the 40-yard line?"

As mentioned earlier, this is obviously a ridiculous conversation. In reality, you would probably get misinformation at best and most likely a phone slammed in your ear if you tried to conduct this conversation. Why? Because it is inherently a win-lose situation —not a win-win situation. Consider, however, if you were the Red Raiders coach and you could ask those questions of the Longhorns coach and get honest, accurate answers, would you ask them? Of course you would!

Is It Win-Lose or Win-Win?

Learn to recognize the difference between win-lose and win-win situations. You cannot convert something that is inherently a win-lose situation, such as a poker game, into a win-win situation. When you sit down to play poker, someone is going to leave the table with more money at someone else's expense. Therefore, the players do not let each other know what cards they're holding. In fact, they deliberately attempt to mislead each other.

Most people tend to think they are in win-lose situations, and, consequently, they don't look for win-win opportunities. They actually create win-lose situations out of win-win situations. For example, is a marriage a win-win situation? Can it be converted to a win-lose relationship? Consider the relationship between a boss and a subordinate—shouldn't it be win-win? Can it become a win-lose situation? Absolutely! Is the relationship between a business and a customer win-win? It should be, but can it deteriorate into win-lose? Once a boss, subordinate, customer, spouse, or anyone thinks he or she is in a win-lose situation, there is a high probability for problems in the relationship. These problems appear because most people do not care to see others gain at their expense. The challenge is to look for and maintain win-win situations. As discussed in the next section, people will answer the "*Red Raiders*" questions in win-win situations.

Take a minute and go back to the very beginning of Chapter 1. Notice that I used probing as a way to show Dick and John that their viewpoints on politics were not nearly as win-lose as they thought.

All Statements Can Become Questions, Can't They?

As illustrated in the sub-title above, you can convert almost anything you want to say to someone into a question. When you pose a question, some very interesting dynamics occur. For purposes of comparison, let's observe two conversations.

Suppose I visit Susan, the vice president of finance at the Widget Manufacturing Company, and during our discussion I say, "You know, Susan, you ought to have your financial analysts using spreadsheet software on their personal computers [PCs]." Alternatively I might say, "Susan, have you ever thought about having your financial analysts use spreadsheet software on their PCs?" Is there any difference in the way the two might affect you if you were Susan? Does Susan think more favorably toward me when I make a statement and put myself in the position of being the expert, or when I ask a question, and put her in the expert position?

Let's consider how Susan might respond. When I state, "You know Susan, you ought to have your financial analysts using spreadsheet software on their PCs," she might reply, "Absolutely not! My friend Robert tried that at his company and it was a disaster!" Am I in trouble? You bet! I committed myself with a statement. I've set up a win-lose situation.

Now, consider how the conversation might proceed if instead I question, "Susan, have you ever thought about having your financial analysts use spreadsheet software on their PCs?" Again she replies, "Absolutely not! My friend Robert tried that at his company and it was a disaster!" Am I in trouble now? No, because I never said she should use PCs and spreadsheets. I just asked if she had ever thought about doing so. Now, what recourse do I have? I can stay in the conversation by asking, "Really, what happened?" Will Susan answer that question? Most likely, because she won't feel like I'm challenging her or trying to put her on the spot. It's still a win-win situation.

In fact, the conversation might go something like this:

"Well," Susan explains, "Robert said that the software worked fine, but the computers they were using just weren't reliable. They kept breaking down."

"What kind of PCs were they using?"

"TAC ZEROs."

Oh? I've never heard of them.

Yeah, well I think TAC stands for Take a Chance, but they're available at a really low price!

"If they had used a computer that was reliable, do you think the outcome would have been different?"

"Probably so."

"If we could find some equipment that was reliable, would you like to explore the possibility of using spreadsheet software on PCs in your department?"

"Well, I would have to be convinced that the equipment was reliable."

"What would it take to convince you?"

"Well, I would have to visit an organization where such an implementation was successful and see for myself."

"If we could locate such a site, would you schedule a visit?"

"Certainly."

Notice that all I did was ask questions. The key is to ask questions in a way that recognizes and acknowledges the other person's intelligence and shows that you are interested in what the other person has to say. If the person perceives the situation as win-win, the *Red Raiders* questions usually get answered.

Why Don't We Ask More Questions?

While the question is the single most powerful communication tool we have, we rarely use it. We are too busy making statements to prove that we are experts rather than asking questions.

Have you ever watched really effective executives? Instead of saying, "George, I need to talk to you in my office right away!" they phrase the request, "George, there are some things we need to discuss. When you have a chance would you drop by my office?" If you're George, you can translate "when you have a chance would you drop by my office?" to mean, 'Unless you have chains around your ankles, I want to see your elbows pumping down the hallway now!' Isn't it nicer, however, to be asked to "drop by"?

The phrasing can make all the difference, can't it? For example, compare "Hand that to me!" with "Would you hand that to me?" Do you see the difference? By switching to a question, the speaker may use a different tone of voice, the listener perceives a different tone, and, most probably, the response or reaction is positive rather than negative or defensive.

Let's consider an issue with which managers are often faced —discussing job performance with subordinates. The following is an example of the communication between me, the manager, and Jane, the employee, who I have summoned to my office.

"Come in, Jane. Have a seat. I want to speak with you for a few moments, because we are very concerned about your performance. I understand that you have done poorly on several past assignments and that you have not been keeping regular hours. You have been reporting to work late as well as sometimes taking up to three hours for your lunch break. Your poor performance coupled with irregular work hours has really become a serious problem." Does this sound like a diplomatic enough start? Upon initial consideration, it may seem okay. But what if Jane responds, "I'm really sorry I have been gone so much. My husband is terminally ill with cancer and that's why I've taken so much time off. I want to be with him as much as I can."

If you're the manager, how would you feel? Do you comprehend the jeopardy you put yourself in when you make statements rather than ask questions? In the previous example, did I perceive that I was dealing with a win-win or win-lose situation. Did my approach allow for it to be anything but win-lose or even lose-lose? Wouldn't it have been better to start the conversation with "How are things going?" "How are things at work?" "How are things at home?" "How do you feel about your performance on your last few assignments?" This would allow me to find out valuable information before committing myself.

Can You Fire Someone by Just Asking Questions?

Having to terminate someone from an organization is probably the most unpleasant task of a manager. However, if the process is controlled by using effective questions, the task can be made at least palatable.

Several years ago, I was the director of a large information systems and data processing center at a state university. One of the employees, Dan (fictitious name), who worked as a computer operator on the swing shift (4:00 p.m. to midnight), had permission from the manager of the computer center to swap shifts with a day shift employee every Thursday because Dan (allegedly) received kidney dialysis treatments on Thursday evenings.

The truth was, Dan was really going bowling every Thursday evening and had lied about needing the kidney dialysis treatment. Someone on the day shift happened to see him bowling one Thursday night and reported it to the computer center manager. Upon closer review, there were several areas where Dan had failed to perform, even after counseling and warnings. Because Dan's manager previously had problems handling such situations, I had to deal with the employee.

How could I begin my conversation with Dan? I could say, "Look, Dan, I know about the bowling on Thursday night!" I didn't want to do that, however, because I had no real evidence. If you accuse someone of something he or she did not do, you risk doing irreparable damage to a relationship. (Besides, maybe Dan has a brother that looks just like him.)

So I asked him, "Dan, would you review for me the arrangement you have for switching shifts on Thursday nights?" (Did he know that I knew about the lie? Sure he did. I had not accused him, but he knew that he had better be honest with me.)

"Actually, I'm on a bowling league on Thursday nights."

"Did you know that your co-workers are aware of this?"

"No," he replied. Then he added, "Well, I figured something was up because you wanted to see me."

"How do you think your co-workers feel about this situation?"

"I guess they are pretty ticked off."

"Do they have a right to be angry, Dan?"

"Yeah, they do."

"Well, they know, your boss knows, and I know. They also know that we are having this meeting and it creates quite a dilemma for me. What do you think they expect me to do?"

"Well, I suppose they expect you to fire me."

"Have you learned from this experience, Dan?"

"Yes, I have!"

"You know, former President Nixon made a mistake that was so serious that he couldn't go anywhere without people remembering it (this situation was right after Watergate). You have made a serious mistake; however, if you learn from this mistake, it can be overcome. Do you think if you had a fresh start working someplace else you could avoid making this kind of mistake again?"

"I realize I *screwed up* big time and really destroyed my credibility around here. I'd probably be better off getting a fresh start somewhere else," Dan admitted.

"Well, if you feel a fresh start would give you an opportunity to avoid making this kind of mistake in the future, I am willing to help. What would you like me to do?"

"I'm sure a letter of recommendation is out of the question, but if you wouldn't have anything negative put in my personnel file to haunt me down the road, I would appreciate it."

"Since it appears that you are going to learn from your mistake, I'll see what I can do to minimize any negative impact on your personnel file," I responded.

Be as diplomatic as you can be when faced with having to fire someone. In this situation, asking questions enabled me to take what would normally be a win-lose situation and keep it as win-win as possible under the circumstances.

Do You Use the Communication Models All the Time?

One of the questions most frequently asked about these communication models is, "How do you learn to think in terms of the models all of the time?" And, the answer is, "You don't!" When conducting casual conversation or small talk with family or friends, you usually don't use the models.

The time to use the models is when you are going to engage in an important conversation (i.e., with your boss, a key customer, an employee), and at other times when a discussion could degenerate into confrontation. Then it becomes very important that you communicate well—when you need to turbo-charge your communication. When you are in disagreement, it becomes worthwhile and necessary to put forth the extra effort to communicate effectively.

The models can also be very effective in helping you prepare for a situation that could easily lead to a misunderstanding or a disaster and permanently damage a relationship. By reading Part Four, "Putting It All Together," you gain insight on how to apply these communication models.

Questions Are Free

Although I know these models very well, I don't use them all the time. The one thing I have programmed myself to do naturally is ask more questions, but I still make mistakes. Just a short time ago, I was involved in a consulting project with a group of top executives from a large company. We were working with strategic planning issues and one guy really made a good impression on me. I thought he was very sharp and made some good points during the day's session.

One evening at dinner with Mark, the director of corporate information systems, I remarked, "I was really impressed by David's comments today. He really understands the business. In fact, with his vision, he'd make a great chief executive officer!" Mark gave me a strange look and commented, "Are you kidding? Nobody in the company can stand that guy!"

(Gulp!) I made a statement without thinking—and I knew better. What should I have done? The correct approach with Mark would have been, "So, what do you think of David?" When Mark declared, "He's a loser! He's pushy and nobody that I know likes him," I would have known to say nothing. No harm, no foul - because **questions are free**.

Questions are Free for Billionaires Too

I was honored to serve on the Board of Directors of the Best Buy Company for fourteen years. Rated by Forbes in 2004 as the best managed company in America, the founder was billionaire Dick Schulze. He had a high school education, but I learned more about business from him than any business professor.

How could he enjoy such incredible success without a business degree? He answered that question for me one day in 1994. During a board meeting, I asked what Best Buy was doing about a web page. Now this was early on in the days of the Internet and web pages were still fairly new. Dick turned and looked at me and in front of the entire Board and asked without hesitation (or embarrassment), "What's a web page?"

In that instant I realized how a guy with a high school education could learn enough to become a multi-billionaire and a leading entrepreneur. He knew (if you weren't afraid to ask in front of others) questions are indeed free as is what you can learn by asking them.

Clearly, it never crossed Dick's brilliant mind what people would think if he didn't know what a web page was. Rather, he was totally confident, as he should have been, that a question was the quickest way to resolve his unfamiliarity with what I was talking about. He was not stupid, just not yet informed. He fixed that problem by simply asking a question.

Sixteen or Sixty and Sociable

In Chapter 3, *Communicating Has Fundamentals Too*, in the section, *Sixteen and Shy*, I discussed social situations and how shyness is frequently misunderstood or interpreted as arrogance. I mentioned then that I would share some techniques you can use to overcome shyness and fear of rejection. Besides being the single most powerful communication tool you can use, the *question* is also the most important socializing tool you can use.

Generally, people like to either talk about themselves or their interests don't they? Effective use of direct probes can get a conversation started, while use of indirect probes can keep a conversation going. So, base your questions on subjects that are of interest to others. One of the original masters of using probing techniques was the late Johnny Carson when he hosted the *Tonight Show* on NBC. The next time you watch one of the better talk shows, pay particular attention to how the host phrases questions.

Psychiatrists may be the elite at probing. Years of dedication to studying and learning prepare them to primarily ask questions. Knowing what to ask and how to interpret the answer enables psychiatrists to help others.

What's really amazing is how other people's perceptions of you can be influenced by social conversation. Not too long ago, I was seated next to a colleague, Vince, on a flight to the west coast. At the time, I was considering buying a sailboat, but I knew very little about sailing a boat or maintaining one. Knowing that Vince owned a sailboat and was an avid sailing enthusiast, I asked him a few questions about the subject, and he gave me a lot of valuable information in a couple of hours.

One week later, I was having lunch with a mutual friend of ours, Gary, who said, "I was talking with Vince the other day and he told me that you are a big-time sailor!" At first I was surprised, but then I realized what had happened. Though my conversation with Vince was one-sided—with him doing most of the talking—his perception was that I really knew a lot about sailing because we talked about it for so long.

Whether you are a teenager, a senior citizen, or somewhere in-between, find out what other people's interests are and then simply use probing techniques to improve your social life.

Increasing Your Impact

While the application of fundamental **verbal** skills is essential to your ability to communicate effectively, your impact can increase dramatically by incorporating the appropriate **non-verbal** communication skills discussed in Part Three.

PART THREE

Non-Verbal Communication Skills

11   *It Goes Without Saying*
12   *Interpreting Body Language*

*Understanding that process preempts content is the key to learning
how to recognize and use non-verbal communication skills.*

11

It Goes Without Saying

In Part One of this book, we discussed the two primary elements of communication, **content** and **process,** pointing out that the process you use to communicate conveys the stronger message of the two. Content is **what** a conversation is about—the subject matter. Process is **how** you conduct the conversation. Understanding that process preempts content is the key to learning how to recognize and use non-verbal communication skills.

Research and clinical studies on the revealing and sometimes contradictory non-verbal messages sent through behavioral patterns or body language have led to a relatively new science called kinesics. Derived from kinesiology, the science or study of human muscular movements, kinesics also considers the communication aspects of bodily movements. For learning and applying the science of kinesics to improve interpersonal communication skills, we focus on how body language impacts the process of communication.

First Impressions

First impressions are an interesting phenomenon. Our first impression of someone is frequently conveyed through non-verbal communications. When we first meet people, their **body language, dress, facial expressions**, and **hands** send messages that form the basis of how we perceive them—often before we get a chance to converse. "Some Enchanted Evening" from the musical *South Pacific* is just one of the many songs written about love *at first sight*—the ultimate in first impressions without a word being spoken.

One element of first impressions is **body language**. Body language is based on body posture, structure, overall conditioning, and movement. These elements, individually and collectively influence the non-verbal messages people convey and the first impressions of other people. For example, a person presenting a seminar on diet and exercise is more convincing if he or she is in good physical condition and has good posture.

Another first impression element is **dress perception**. Dress perception is based upon a combination of style, cleanliness, and appropriateness for the occasion. If you were to attend one of my seminars on developing interpersonal skills and I wore black leather pants, motorcycle riding boots, and a Harley-Davidson T-shirt during the entire seminar, what would be your first impression of me? Inappropriate dress can send a message that overwhelms content to the point where the intended message is completely lost.

Style and cleanliness of clothing can also have an impact, even if one is dressed appropriately. Some professors I know have so much food on their neckties that they could take up a collection of them, boil them in hot water and make soup! Do you think such an appearance might distract from the message when presenting to a polished business executive?

Facial expression also sends a message. This element is primarily conveyed by eye and mouth movements and expressions, e.g., puppy dog eyes, a frown, a grin from ear to ear. (Some people can move their ears, but that is generally not functional for communication purposes!)

Like the face, **hands** can also send a message by the way they are positioned, adorned, and groomed. In the 1950s, the Russian leader Khrushchev's clenched fist and pounding shoe ushered in the 30 years of the Cold War. The open, cupped, extended two hands reaching under and rescuing the house and family perishing in flood waters conveys the primary advertising slogan of Allstate Insurance.

This *first impression package* that we register with other people, based upon the above non-verbal messages, has three aspects:

1. Time extension
2. Resemblance to someone familiar
3. Categorization

I'll Remember You

Time extension is the lasting impact that a first impression has on us. For example, suppose you attend my seminar and I am dressed appropriately, but my pants are unzipped and I speak for two hours before taking a break, only to realize I have forgotten to zip up my pants. Two years from now when someone asks if you remember Wetherbe's seminar, you will probably laugh and say, "Yes I sure do! I'll never forget it! I remember he sure was embarrassed when he found out his pants were unzipped!" What a first impression!

Have you ever worked in an organization where a new employee was absent because of illness for three or four days during the first week on the job? What's the rap on the new person? 'He's always sick.' Even though he may not miss any work due to illness for the rest of the year, the first impression still lingers. First impressions, particularly negative first impressions, require extensive counter behavior to reverse.

The First Time Ever I Saw Your Face

Resemblance to someone familiar, a first impression based mostly on facial appearance, is a first impression beyond your control. In a developing relationship, however, it may be useful to find out the impression your new friend or associate has of the person you resemble. Was your look-alike someone the other person cared for, e.g., an old flame? Or, was your look-alike someone he or she despised? This information can help you decide whether you should be cautious, assertive, matter-of-fact, etc., with your new acquaintance.

Several years ago, I worked with a man at an oil company who could have won a look-alike contest with the comedian and actor, Steve Martin. This fellow was an internal auditor and very conscientious about his job. But it was almost impossible for him to do his job effectively because nobody took him seriously. When he came to my office (or the offices of other people), sat down, and began auditing, we thought he was putting us on. We kept waiting for him to crack a joke and break into a Steve Martin imitation. He finally had to transfer into another position.

Stereotypes

Categorization deals with *putting people into boxes*. We tend to categorize people based on their interests, where they work, their professions, and the hobbies they enjoy. Have you ever experienced instant affiliation when meeting someone for the first time, on an airplane for example, by finding out he or she was in the same profession? Do you develop a general impression of someone when you find out that he or she is a physician, lawyer, university professor, Internal Revenue Service auditor? Occasionally I have wondered how my neighbors would treat me if I worked for the IRS.

As we develop initial impressions of people, first by physical attributes and second by conversation, we make associations with our past experiences, knowledge, and understanding. Since playwrights understand this, one of the things they do when writing a script for a play is to use the behavior of the characters to send a message through our observations. If a character is seen helping a little old lady cross a street, then giving some money to a pauper, the playwright is creating a character image of a generous person in our minds. To convey that a character is a dishonest shyster, *Mr. Shody Toadster* may be seen leaving his table in a restaurant and discretely pocketing a tip left on another table. Through each of these instances, the viewers begin making some judgments about the characters.

Since developing these impressions through the script can be lengthy, guess what playwrights do to save time? They take advantage of our stereotypes. For instance, instead of having *Mr. Gotta Realdeal*, a used car salesman, display several dishonest deeds to establish his role, he may simply have slicked-back hair and wear a loud necktie and a plaid sports jacket. Such character-ization makes the same point in far less time, given the stereotype that most people have of slick, fast-talking, used-car salesmen.

Playwrights leverage the job a person has, something about his or her background, or some physical attribute to save dialogue time in a play. Since we all have biases and stereotypes developed over time, playwrights capitalize on these to deliver their message.

Credibility

As stereotyping can influence first impressions, so can one's credibility. Credibility is critical when you are trying to communicate effectively. Having credibility means that you are worthy of confi-dence, reliable, and capable of being believed. Just where does credibility come from and how can it be maintained?

Credibility comes from:

1. Having knowledge or expertise
2. Being trustworthy
3. Being dynamic
4. Having status or rank

An interesting observation about these sources of credibility is that some are situation-specific while the others are more general in nature.

Expertise

Expertise is a situation-specific source of credibility. For exam-ple, we may have a discussion about information systems design and development techniques and you decide that I am knowledgeable in that area. Later on, we may be talking about fishing, something I don't know much about, and I might ask, "Why does a fish ever bite a hook in the first place?"

"You don't know about bait?"

"What's bait?" (I'm not really that ignorant about fishing.)

Would the fact that I know little about fishing, however, take away from my expertise in information systems development? No, not at all, because expertise is situation-specific. I can be an expert in one area and not in another unrelated area and still maintain credibility with you when discussing the subject of which I am knowledgeable.

Trust Me

Unlike expertise, trustworthiness is not situation-specific; rather, it is a general area of credibility. Suppose we have lunch together, and as we leave the restaurant I pass a table with a tip on it and slip the tip into my pocket. "Easy money," I whisper to you.

An hour later in the seminar you are attending, I say, "Trust me, if you learn these communication models you can be more persuasive, avoid arguments..." You might be thinking to yourself, 'Am I going to believe a guy who stole a tip? No way!' If you perceive me to be dishonest either by my actions or through misrepresenting myself by claiming to be an expert in an area that I know nothing about, then you may not believe anything I tell you and feel I am not credible.

Dynamism

Being dynamic is the third aspect of being credible. Enthusiastic, intense people are more believable than those who are not very dynamic. Politics aside, one big advantage Ronald Reagan had over Jimmy Carter during their campaigns for president of the United States was Reagan's enthusiasm. Reagan simply was much more dynamic in his speaking and discussions about the issues. The same advantage applied to Bill Clinton when he defeated Robert Dole. Note that like expertise, dynamism tends to be situation-specific. Being enthusiastic all of the time might be beneficial, but it is not very realistic. However, enthusiasm is critical when one is trying to be convincing and credible.

Rank and File

Finally, credibility, as it pertains to rank or status, tends to transcend situations. Your rank or status in an organization or communicating situation has an impact on your credibility. For instance, when someone questions, "Who said we had to do that?" and the response is, "The CEO, that's who!"—heels click, hands salute, and voices ring out, "Yes, Sir!"

The Four Corners of Credibility

Pretend you have read a story about me in the newspaper relating how I found a bank deposit bag along the side of the road containing several thousand dollars. The deposit slip in the bag indicated the money belonged to a retirement home, so I returned the money to the director of the home. Based on that incident, you believe that I am honest and trustworthy.

Some weeks later, you hear me introduced at a conference by the master of ceremonies as an author and an expert in project management. Animatedly and enthusiastically I begin speaking about project management, using dynamic gestures. Then someone in the audience asks me to explain how to develop a work breakdown structure. In trying to answer, I mumble and speak in generalities. It becomes clear to the audience that I don't know what I'm talking about. Am I in trouble from a credibility standpoint as you decide, 'Hmm, I don't think this guy knows what he's talking about?'

Now let's change the situation slightly. Let's pretend I do answer the question and it is clear that I know my subject matter. However, three people in the audience saw me steal a tip during lunch and told everyone about it. Do I have any credibility problems with you or other members of the audience?

Again, let's change the scenario. Suppose I didn't steal the tip, you trust me, I'm introduced as a leading expert, and I clearly know what I'm talking about. However, when I speak, I just stand there, head down, talking slowly as if I'm bored to death ... "So anyway folks, project management is important to the welfare of the computer department and to the company (yawn). I've been using it a long time and, ah, I like it." Have I got a problem?

Now, pretend that the master of ceremonies says, "I am pleased to introduce Mr. Wetherbe, the presenter of today's seminar. He is currently a freshman at the university." Even though I speak enthusiastically and knowledgeably about project management, you probably would be thinking during the entire seminar, 'Freshman? What is this?'

These examples illustrate why all four sources of credibility are integral to ensuring effective communication. They also demonstrate that by *blowing* any one of the four sources of credibility - **BOOM!**—credibility is lost and effective communication is hindered.

The Communication Puzzle

We communicate in different ways. The obvious way is with words and numbers, the literal aspects of communication. The non-verbal aspects, however, play a key role in communicating. In addition to body language, non-verbal communication is also based on the use of:

1. Silence
2. Voice inflection
3. Facial expressions
4. Noise
5. Touch

If you were to ask me, for instance, "What do you think about Bob's contribution to the project?" the perception of my response can vary widely even though I use the same content.

Consider the following examples.

"Bob contributed." An immediate, **direct response** implies that I was pleased with Bob's contribution and felt it was satisfactory.

However, if I responded, "[long pause] Bob contributed," the prolonged *silence* before the answer actually has a reversing effect. A long pause before an answer generally conveys the opposite of what is being said.

If you have had any prior experience interacting with children, you may have encountered a situation like this: "Did you break that lamp, Joey?" Joey pauses for a long time and then responds, "No". That hesitation is a dead giveaway that you aren't getting the whole story.

Voice inflection can also have a significant impact on the message. "Bob [raised voice] contributed [lower voice]." The voice inflection in this case implies a minimal effort on the part of Bob.

Facial expressions can be an indication that there is more to the message than just what was said. "[Upward look as though searching for an answer] Bob contributed." The thoughtful "search" for the right answer, in this case, indicates a less than satisfactory effort on the part of Bob. Rubbing an eyebrow or scratching an ear while answering implies the same message.

Noise such as a sigh, whistle, or audible yawn certainly conveys a message. "Bob [loud sigh] contributed." This response casts doubt on the significance of Bob's contribution.

Gently *touching* the upper arm or forearm of the person with whom you are communicating as you answer in a sympathetic way, "Bob contributed," sends a message that Bob's contribution wasn't much, but he did the best he could.

Reading the Signals

As you can see from the previous discussions, there are many factors that can totally alter the message. A question can come across as either, "I am challenging you," or "I would like to learn." A response can come across as, "Gee, I am happy to share this with you," or "How can you be so stupid as to ask such a question?" Non-verbal signals can either enhance or contradict words and numbers, making a big difference in communication. Those differences are discussed in greater detail in Chapter 12.

By combining a positive non-verbal signal with the use of the appropriate verbal communication model, you can dramatically increase the power and effectiveness of your message.

12

Interpreting Body Language

Even if you have had no training, you probably know a great deal about how to interpret body language signals. Usually, by just paying attention, you can intuitively understand body language. Sometimes words mean nothing. Sometimes they mean everything.

Have you ever made a comment and someone else replies, "You don't mean that." And you say, "What do you mean I don't mean that. I just said it, didn't I?" What happened is that the other person was aware of your body language or other signals that conveyed the opposite of what you said.

What's Going on in That Phone Booth?

Here is a little body language quiz for you. Before reading any further, study the three examples of someone talking on the telephone in Figure 12.1.

1   **2**   **3**

Figure 12.1 BODY LANGUAGE MATCH QUIZ

Match each of the three with the following choices based on their body language.

       a: Husband   _2_

       b: Lover   _3_

       c: Salesman   _1_

OK, let's see if your impression matches what was intended. Picture 1 is the *salesman*. He's saying, "All right, I'll get that shipment to you next week."

Picture 2 is the *husband*. He's standing rather relaxed saying, "OK, you want me to pick up a carton of milk, a loaf of bread, and what else dear?"

Picture 3 is the *lover*. He's whispering, "I can hardly wait *sugar lips*. I'll meet you tonight at 8:00."

Body language can speak volumes.

Silhouettes on the Shade

The next body language quiz is a little more difficult because you have extraordinarily limited information: No movement, no facial expression, no sound—just a silhouette. Study each one before reading further.

1   2   3   4   5   6

Figure 12.2 SILHOUETTE MATCH QUIZ

Try to match each silhouette (1 through 6) with the labels (a through f) listed below.

a: Openness, Looking for Acceptance _____

b: Relaxed Negativism _____

c: Lecture _____

d: Headache _____

e: Closed Acceptance, Defiance _____

f: Aggressiveness _____

Now let's see how well you did. Some of these are tricky because the differences are very subtle.

> ***Openness*** is silhouette 5. Her arms are in an open, accepting position with palms facing forward and upward.
>
> ***Relaxed negativism*** is silhouette 4. Arms are crossed and he is leaning slightly backwards.
>
> ***Lecture*** is silhouette 1. By the way, finger pointing is generally not a good practice.
>
> ***Headache*** is silhouette 3. I'll bet you got this one correct.
>
> ***Closed acceptance*** is silhouette 2. This one is easy to confuse with aggressiveness. The difference is in the width of the stance and the placement of the hands on the hips.
>
> ***Aggressiveness*** is silhouette 6. Hands on the hips and a wide stance indicates that this person is ready to do battle.

Body language messages do communicate.

Body Language: A Short Skills Course

There are several key non-verbal messages to help facilitate your communication process. These messages work in concert with the verbal communication models and are essential to developing effective interpersonal skills.

You can enhance your communication skills if you can recognize, understand, and master the positive non-verbal signals of *openness, reassurance, cooperation, confidence,* and *acceptance.* By combining a positive non-verbal signal with the use of the appropriate verbal communication model, you can dramatically increase the power and effectiveness of your message.

Of equal importance is the ability to recognize, understand, and counter the negative non-verbal signals of *defensiveness, suspicion, frustration, nervousness,* and *boredom.*

The following 10 figures present a graphic illustration of each of the above key non-verbal signals or messages. Accompanying each figure is a list of the significant attributes to look for and understand when interpreting the meaning of non-verbal signals.

Figures 12.3 through 12.7 illustrate non-verbal messages for you to learn to project and portray during the communication process. Study each of the illustrations and their corresponding discussions.

Figure 12.3 OPENNESS

Directly facing
Forward lean
Good eye contact
Spread legs (except women sitting in a dress)
Open/exposed palms
Open coat or jacket

An example of an effective time to use the non-verbal message of *openness* is while using the **Explanation Model**. Use the two together to more effectively persuade your listener that your solution is the best answer to the problem. Openness should be your overall, dominant, non-verbal message, particularly when dealing with conflict or when probing.

Figure 12.4 REASSURANCE

Raised eyebrows (puppy-dog eyes)
Hands to chest (men)
Hands to lower neck (women)

The non-verbal expression of *reassurance* is most effective when using the **Reservation/Doubt Model**. When providing reassurance and substantiation you do not want to appear argumentative or defensive in substantiating your position or solution.

105

Figure 12.5 COOPERATION

Everything to convey openness
  plus
Remove coat or jacket
Roll up sleeves
Illustrate the "scales of justice" with open hands

Sending the message that you are offering *cooperation* is effective with several verbal models. For example, when using the **Question/Confusion/Conflict Model**, the *scales of justice* gesture gives the indication that you are weighing one thing against another. By holding your arms somewhat outstretched with your palms facing upward, you can add emphasis when you say, "On one hand we incur more cost, but on the other hand, we save a substantial amount of time."

Figure 12.6 CONFIDENCE

Erect, relaxed posture
Minimal blinking of eyes
Steeple fingers (low)

The non-verbal message reflecting *confidence* works well with the **Explanation Model** and the **Closure Model**. Form a <u>low</u> steeple with the fingers as shown in the illustration. Be careful to keep your hands low. If your hands are held high in a steepled position, the message may be interpreted as arrogance.

Figure 12.7 ACCEPTANCE

Mirror the other person's body position
Relaxed body posture
Turn toward the person
Display an open posture

Have you ever noticed how two people who appear to be very comfortable with each other position themselves when conversing? They frequently assume the same position; that is, they *mirror* each other. When you mirror someone else's standing or sitting position or notice that someone with whom you are conversing has mirrored your position, it's a good sign that you have achieved acceptance. The **Query** and **Closure Models** are two examples where *acceptance* is effective as a non-verbal message.

Learn to Counter These

Figures 12.8 through 12.12 illustrate non-verbal messages you should learn to recognize and counter. Interpreting body language is not a perfected science. Nevertheless, a basic understanding of the potential meaning of signals projected through body language can provide clues to attitudes and feelings that can be explored and verified with effective verbal communication. Study these next five figures and learn to identify potentially negative signals.

One important aspect of countering negative non-verbal messages is knowing how to verify that a negative signal is, in fact, being sent. The probe is the key to verifying non-verbal messages you receive. By asking questions, you can obtain the content you need to confirm non-verbal signals.

Equally important is learning to avoid sending negative, non-verbal signals. Many times we say one thing and unknowingly send a non-verbal message that conveys just the opposite. Study the following illustrations and their corresponding discussions.

Figure 12.8 DEFENSIVENESS

Arms crossed
Legs crossed
Hands clenched
Body turned away while maintaining eye contact
Rearward lean

An important consideration when interpreting any non-verbal message is the presence of corresponding gestures. For example, people frequently cross their arms and legs because they are cold rather than being defensive. The key is to use people's body language as a clue to what they might be thinking. If someone is sending a message of *defensiveness* while expressing *reservation or doubt*, then you may have more to overcome than meets the eye.

Figure 12.9 SUSPICION

Covering mouth with non-dominant hand
Touching or stroking ear or earlobe
Touching or stroking eyebrow
Covering face and eyes with hands

When you see your listener cover his or her mouth with the non-dominant hand, (e.g., a *right-hander* placing the left hand over his or her mouth) it may be a sign of *suspicion*. When someone covers his mouth while listening to you, he may be thinking, 'This is *baloney*'. Finger-stroking of the ear, eyebrow, or nose is usually not an indication of suspicion; more likely, doubt is being expressed. When someone covers his face and eyes with his hands it's like he is saying, "I just don't see it." If any of these signs occur but nothing is said, you may want to switch to the **Query Model** and use a direct probe such as, "Do you have any thoughts about what I've said so far?"—to gain some content.

Figure 12.10 FRUSTRATION

Hunched forward
Knurled brow
Clasped hands
Emotional look

An indication of frustration could mean that the person you are conversing with has severe conflict with what you are saying, or it could simply mean that he has something else on his mind. For example, your boss could be running late for an important appointment and you are just making things worse with your explanation. When you sense frustration on the part of your listener, probe for content, then deal with it using the appropriate model. Alternatively, postpone your conversation to a time that is more convenient for your listener.

Figure 12.11 NERVOUSNESS

Wringing of hands
Twitchy movements
Blinking eyes
Fidgety movement
Swiveling in chair

An indication of nervousness could just be a personal attribute or it could be an indication that the person you are speaking with is very uncomfortable with what you are proposing. Again, the key here is to query with an indirect probe, followed with a direct probe, if necessary, to obtain content for guiding your response.

Figure 12.12 BOREDOM

Foot and/or finger tapping
Face resting in hand, plus
Drowsiness or drowsy look

A person indicating signs of boredom can easily be confused with someone who is tired, especially if he is resting his face in his hand or appears drowsy. If you feel that your listener is losing interest in what you are talking about, get him or her involved in the conversation by asking a question. An indirect probe such as, "Do you have any questions or concerns about what I've said so far?" helps your listener focus on what you are saying.

Keep Things in Perspective

Remember that the body language, voice inflection, facial expressions, and other non-verbal signs of communication we are discussing in this book are based on Western culture. Expressions in many Asian, East Indian, and Polynesian cultures may take on completely different meanings. When you are interacting on an international basis, study the cultural characteristics of the nationality with which you are dealing. Probe to find out differences between cultures with which you are familiar and those with which you are not for possible body language messages.

Application of Positive Body Language Messages

As discussed in Figures 12.3 through 12.7, each of the positive body language messages can be combined with several of the verbal communication models. Table 12.1 provides a summary of where to apply primary and secondary usage of positive body language signals. For example, when would you convey openness? As illustrated in Table 12.1, you should convey openness most of the time.

When would you want to send a message of reassurance? Reassure when someone expresses reservation or doubt. For example, use the non-verbal message of reassurance when you say, "Well, we certainly wouldn't want someone who wasn't qualified handling the payroll transactions."

Then add a non-verbal message of confidence when you substantiate with, "I personally know of two previous times when John handled payroll processing by himself. You can certainly count on him again."

If you don't have hard facts to substantiate your recommendation of John to process the payroll transactions, you might continue to project reassuring body language as you explain, "John has not yet had the opportunity to process the payroll transactions on his own; however, I have observed him assisting others, and I can assure you that you will not be disappointed with his performance."

Table 12.1 VERBAL COMMUNICATION and POSITIVE BODY LANGUAGE INTERACTION CHART

BODY LANGUAGE Primary = **P** Secondary = **S** *VERBAL COMMUNICATION*	OPENNESS	REASSURANCE	COOPERATION	CONFIDENCE	ACCEPTANCE
QUERY					
Indirect Probe	P				S
Direct Probe	P				S
EXPLANATION					
Problem	P				
Solution	P		S	S	
AGREEMENT					
Reinforce	P		S		
Expand	P		S	S	S
RESERVATION/DOUBT					
Reassure	S	P			
Substantiate	P	S		S	
QUESTION/CONFUSION/CONFLICT					
Rephrase	P				S
Answer/Clarify/Minimize	P		S		
CLOSURE					
Review Points of Agreement	P		S		S
Propose Course of Action	P		S	S	S

In this case, the hands-to-chest gesture conveys, 'Believe me because of my trustworthiness, not because I can prove it.'

Sending a message of cooperation is very important during the solution part of your explanation. Cooperative body language also helps you convey a message of cooperation and minimize conflict. For example, when you say, "We have to ask ourselves, what will be more upsetting to upper management: 1) a $250 overrun in the overtime account, or 2) 10,000 people complaining because they did not get their paychecks?" use the *scales of justice* expression with your hands as if you are weighing one alternative against the other.

Acceptance works well with openness. As with openness, try to project acceptance most of the time. When someone leans forward when talking to you, you should lean forward also. If someone you are conversing with is not mirroring your actions or posture, it may be because he or she is uncomfortable with you and does not feel relaxed. You must consider that in the context of your discussion and adjust to make the other person feel more at ease.

Countering Negative Body Language Messages In Others

As depicted in Figures 12.8 through 12.12, defensiveness, suspicion, frustration, nervousness, and boredom are all negative nonverbal messages you want to be able to recognize in others. If someone looks like he or she is getting suspicious when you are presenting your world-class idea, what model should you use? As illustrated in Table 12.2, the Query Model is the only model to use to verify negative body language signals. Why? Because you do not want to assume that a particular gesture is negative. For example, someone may appear to be bored due to drowsiness, when he or she is actually ill and drowsy from medication.

Table 12.2 VERBAL COMMUNICATION and NEGATIVE BODY LANGUAGE INTERACTION CHART

BODY LANGUAGE Primary = **P** Secondary = **S** *VERBAL COMMUNICATION*	DEFENSIVENESS	SUSPICION	FRUSTRATION	NERVOUSNESS	BOREDOM
QUERY					
Indirect Probe	P	P	P	P	P
Direct Probe	P	P	P	P	P
EXPLANATION					
Problem					
Solution					
AGREEMENT					
Reinforce					
Expand					
RESERVATION/DOUBT					
Reassure					
Substantiate					
QUESTION/CONFUSION/CONFLICT					
Rephrase					
Answer/Clarify/Minimize					
CLOSURE					
Review Points of Agreement					
Propose Course of Action					

When using the Query Model, start with an indirect probe. I don't mean you should say, "I noticed you are covering your mouth with your non-dominant hand. Is something wrong?" Instead, just ask, "What do you think about what I've said so far?" Use the non-verbal signals projected by others to prompt you to probe to see if there is a problem. Continue to probe and read body language signals until you have developed an open dialogue, rich in content, which you can use to accomplish your objective.

'Bozo' the Boss: The Exception to the Rule

You should generally avoid sending negative non-verbal messages. The only time you might want to consider sending or using negative non-verbal messages is in that really awkward situation where you have to say one thing, but mean another. For example, let's say someone asks you what you think of your boss and it's a well known fact that your boss is a real *bozo*. You could respond, "My boss? Everyone knows he's a bozo." That is not a good idea. It could get back to your boss.

Let's suppose that it is the manager of your boss who is asking you this question. He may know that your boss is a *bozo* and he just might be getting confirmation. The fact that you are so ready to admit it may make him think, 'I really wouldn't want this person reporting directly to me. He has no loyalty.' But, on the other hand, if you say, "You mean Bozo? I love Bozo, he's the best boss I've ever had!" you are in trouble, again. Your boss' manager thinks, 'Oh no, I've got to get rid of both of them!'

So, how do you respond? You might start with silence, perhaps stroke your ear (indicating reservation/doubt), and say, "Well, I would have to say that at my level it is really hard for me to make an evaluation. I'm really not in a position to judge."

Along with your vague response, your non-verbal message indicates that you are uneasy with this discussion. Your boss' manager should get the message that you know your boss is a bozo but you don't want to be disloyal. On those rare occasions, such as this, when it is not in your best interest to reinforce your words with actions, you can send mixed signals by sending one message ver-bally and conveying another non-verbally.

Soften Things Up

Have you ever noticed that sometimes people come across harsher than they mean to? Your first impression of someone might be that he is a tough *cookie*, but when you get to know him, he is not that way at all. Have you ever sat next to someone on an airplane who looks like she would bite your head off if you tried to strike up a conversation? Then the airplane runs into some air turbulence and things loosen up; you weakly smile at each other, start a conversation, and find much to discuss. Later you think, 'she really is a friendly person, but she didn't look very friendly when I sat down'.

As a general rule, all of us need to soften the image we project. If you soften your image, you become more approachable. People who are really effective as leaders and communicators are those whom others like and feel comfortable meeting, rather than those who intimidate.

How can you soften your image? Use the letters in the word **SOFTEN** to provide you the keys:

S - Smile. If you smile at people, they are more responsive to you. A good example of the ultimate smiler is the puppy dog. A puppy approaches you with its tail wagging (which is a dog's way of smiling) and you know it's thinking, 'I just like you so much! Please pet me!' When you smile at people, even strangers, they smile back nine times out of ten. Those that don't return your smile probably have their thoughts elsewhere or didn't notice you.

O - Open posture. An open posture goes hand-in-hand with a smile. An open posture combined with a genuinely friendly smile is a great way to diffuse someone who is trying to be negative or defensive toward you.

F - Forward lean. When you lean forward, particularly when sitting, you project more interest and intensity.

T - Touch. Touch people more often. What if you're concerned about harassment or sexual implications by using touch? Well, let's explore touching for a moment. There is *good touching* and there is *bad touching*. A hand shake is considered good. When you meet someone, you frequently shake hands as a gesture of friendship. A pat on the back? Generally considered good, if the touch is light and quick. Quickly and lightly touching the shoulder, upper arm, forearm, and hand are also generally considered acceptable areas to touch—other areas are not.

Suppose we are working on a project together. You come up with an innovative idea and I give you a quick tap on your forearm while I say, "That's great, thanks a lot!" That gesture would be acceptable. There is nothing suggestive or offensive conveyed in that gesture whatsoever. Whether or not you are conscious of it, that quick, light, friendly touch sends a warm, comfortable, 'I am appreciated' feeling to your brain.

Problems can arise with a prolonged touch. Leaving my hand on your forearm or shoulder could be construed to be suggestive. *Bad touching* in the work place is any touching gesture that goes beyond a friendly show of appreciation. If, for any reason, someone jerks away, reacts negatively, or in anyway indicates that he or she prefers not to be touched, avoid touching that person, despite your good intentions.

E - Eye contact. A good rule of thumb is to maintain eye contact with the person with whom you are conversing about 60 percent of the time. Little or no eye contact is generally interpreted as lack of confidence. Eye contact that exceeds 70 percent of the time is usually interpreted as aggressiveness and can be irritating to others. People usually want to look away when they are considering what you have said or what they want to say next. Let them.

N - Nod 'yes'. Nodding 'yes', even in uncomfortable situations, can be an effective means to diffuse hostility. You are conveying,

'Yes, it is OK for you to disagree with me.' Once two people can agree to disagree, without becoming defensive or suspicious, they can proceed with the process of communicating with each other more effectively.

PART FOUR

Putting It All Together

When reflecting on my communication with the dean, I realized nothing significant happened in our conversation that I had not anticipated. Therein lies the power of using the models to analyze and prepare for important meetings or communication events.

13

Case Study: Can't Leave Without a Leave of Absence

This case study is an example of how to prepare for communicating in an important, difficult situation. Jim Wetherbe, one of the authors, tells how he used the communication models presented in this book to manage a conversation that had a very significant impact on his career.

In Jim's Own Words

This was one of the most important communication exercises of my career. First, let me set the stage. The year was 1978, and I was a new assistant professor in the College of Business Administration at the University of Houston. I was a recent Ph.D. graduate with a degree in management information systems (MIS). Because MIS was a relatively new field at the time, there was a national shortage of faculty. There were about two hundred openings for every two or three Ph.D. graduates. I was only the second faculty member in my field at the University of Houston. The university had hired a third faculty member; however, that person was not joining us for a year. In addition to our undergraduate and masters of business administration graduate programs, we were just getting our MIS Ph.D. program started, having accepted two Ph.D. students into the program.

During the school year, one of the most successful oil exploration companies in the United States approached me about working with them. This company was planning on developing its own state-of-the-art computer center and wanted me to be a part of its management team. The company was using a service company to handle all its data processing and computing requirements. However, based on the company's rapid growth and plans for expansion, corporate management decided to transfer all of its computer-related information processing from the data processing service company to an in-house facility to be developed during the coming year—and, money was no object.

Since this was my first year as a professor, I did not want to quit. Working with this company was an exceptional opportunity, however, and I wondered if there was any way I could be a part of the oil exploration company's management team and still maintain my career at the university. Was there a win-win situation? I had heard about something called a *leave-of-absence*. The university employee handbook explained that it was a one-way commitment from the university, allowing a person to go away for a year while guaranteeing his or her job upon return. The handbook indicated a faculty member was entitled to such a leave of absence after six years of service. No exceptions to this guideline were discussed. I would obviously need an exception. Knowing the fundamentals of communication, what would I want to do? Probe!

I asked questions of many people at the university such as, "What do you know about the leave of absence policy here at the university?" Here is what I found out. The applicant submitted a request to his or her department chairperson who forwarded it to the dean. The dean was the person who really made the decision about whether approval was granted, and, in turn, sent the request to the university president for essentially rubber stamp approval.

So, What's Wrong With This Picture?

What negatives (i.e., reservations, doubt, questions, confusion, or conflict) might you anticipate the dean to have if I were to request an immediate leave of absence for a year? See if you can guess before proceeding. I found out by both guessing and asking questions of my close friends on the faculty.

On Committing Professional Suicide

"So, how do you think the dean would view a request for a leave of absence from me?" I asked several of my colleagues. "Don't even ask! He will tell you no," was their reply. "The dean has very strong feelings about organizational loyalty. Your request for a leave of absence after only being here for one year will be perceived as a lack of commitment to the university," was the general consensus. From my colleagues' perspective, I was facing a lose-lose situation. If I went ahead and asked the dean for a leave of absence, he would think I wasn't loyal and was rather stupid for asking him to make an exception after only being there for one year. Unless I was prepared to quit if I couldn't get a leave, the overall recommendation was, "Don't ask!"

However, knowing the communication skills presented in this book—no problem—I could proceed! First I had to decide what were the issues that might create objections and what might he not believe? Then, I could categorize possible responses according to the models into reservations, doubt, questions, confusion, and conflict.

The Case Against Me

The three most likely issues to be raised by the dean were as follows:

1. 'Who will cover your classes?' A valid concern to anticipate is how my classes will be covered if I'm gone. He can't hire someone else; there is no one to hire.

2. 'I don't want to set a precedent for the Office of Administration that I'll have to deal with in the future or justify to the president's office,' is another valid objection that might be raised.

3. 'You may decide not to return after a year.' Again, another valid concern that the dean might express.

If you think about it, these three issues are fairly logical, aren't they? Putting yourself in the dean's position, wouldn't these be your primary concerns?

My task was to figure out how to deal with these concerns. Unless I could come up with some content that I was comfortable with, I would be a fool to ask for a leave of absence. However, if I had some reasonable content, I could explore some alternatives for addressing his concerns and avoid damaging our relationship.

Content From Role Playing

How did I come up with the content to respond to the likely objections? Well, I spent some time thinking about various ways to address each concern and tried them out on some friends through role playing. I took colleagues to lunch and asked for their opinions and reactions to my responses using *what-if* scenarios. When they answered with statements like, "I think that sounds like you are looking out for yourself and don't care much about the university," I'd reconsider, then rephrase my response, and try again.

I probably spent six or seven hours getting ready for this meeting with the dean. I really wanted to work with the company for a year; however, I did not want to jeopardize my position with the university. I had to figure out a way to make it a win-win situation.

Show Time

After thinking through all of the communication models and practicing my responses through role playing, I finally made an appointment with the dean. I went to his office at ten o'clock in the morning. What do you think I should have said to start the conversation?

Here is a good general approach for opening a meeting or an appointment with someone who is higher in the organization hierarchy than you are.

Probe Number One

"Good morning! We had an appointment at ten o'clock. Is this still a good time for you?" If he or she seems distracted and says, "Well, actually I'm trying to get the budget together and I'm running a little late," you want to show consideration by responding with something like, "I know that is important, I can wait." or "Let me reschedule for another time when you're not so busy." (And, I'm out of there! If I'm going to try to pull off the coup of my career, I want to make sure the dean is in the right frame of mind.)

As it turned out, the dean said, "This is a good time, have a seat. Would you like a cup of coffee?"

Probe Number Two

('OK, the *vibes* are right!' I thought to myself, as I sat down.) "How can I help you?" he said. I continued to probe with, "Could you share some information with me about the leave of absence process? What's the philosophy behind it? Basically, how does the arrangement work?" Did I already know the answers to these questions? Of course I did. What I didn't know, however, were his views. I had to assume the responsibility for understanding his point of view, not just what was in the university employee handbook—because he might not value the handbook very much.

The dean responded, "Well, the leave of absence policy is designed to allow faculty members to spend a year doing something to expand their professional knowledge and experience in ways that increase their effectiveness and productivity as an educator and a scholar." (So far, so good.)

Probe Number Three (Part One and Part Two)

Next, I asked, "What are the guidelines for taking a leave of absence?" [part one]. He replied, "The guideline is you are eligible after your sixth year." "Are exceptions to that guideline ever made?" I asked [part two]. The dean said, "I can recall one person who took a leave after three years. That was several years ago, before I became dean here." (Gulp! That didn't sound too promising.)

Probe Number Four

Now here was the pivotal question, "What is your personal view on making exceptions to the guideline?" I asked.

Based on input from my colleagues, here is what I expected him to say, 'Well, the way I look at it, a leave of absence is something you earn after years of dedicated and committed service and I'm not really much in favor of exceptions.' Would I have been in trouble? No, I would simply have said, 'Sounds reasonable to me. Thank you for sharing your perspective with me.' (And then I'm *outta* there!)

There was always the possibility that the dean could have asked at any point, 'Why are you asking these questions?' Keep in mind that I had previously established a good relationship with this person. Also remember, I asked my questions with *puppy-dog eyes* and in the spirit of wanting to learn. Nonetheless, I needed to be prepared in case he questioned me. So prior to this meeting, I had simulated and rehearsed the situation where he asked me why I was asking those questions. Had he done so, he would have forced me into my Explanation Model prematurely.

For the sake of explanation, let's say he asked, "Why all these questions?" I would have explained, "As you know, I'm in the field of MIS and there is so much change occurring with computer technology that it is very difficult to keep current with the state-of-the-art. In fact, many people say that we in academia need to really reach out to the business community through consulting and research because we cannot keep up by staying on campus. **[problem]** A leave of absence is a particularly attractive way to have an immersed relationship with an organization, and I wanted to find out as much as I could about how it works to understand how to exercise the option." **[solution]** Then, I would have immediately asked, "Have any exceptions ever been made?"

You can usually use three or four probes before someone will ask you, "Why all the questions?" In general, my probes were based on:

1. What is it?
2. What is the time guideline?
3. Have any exceptions been made?
4. What is your position?

Any more probes than that and I would have been pushing my luck. Those were the four questions I wanted to get answered. To prepare for these situations, ask yourself, "If I can only ask three or four questions, what would they be and in what order would I ask them?" As it turned out, I got in four probes and he never asked me why I was asking questions (good puppy-dog eyes, I guess).

Hallelujah!

To the fourth probe (i.e., "What is your personal view on making exceptions to the guideline?"), here is the reply he gave: "It's interesting that you should ask. I've seen a lot of faculty members come up on their sixth year who wanted to exercise the leave of absence option, but there were no real good opportunities available. However, many of them went ahead and took it anyway, just because it was available rather than for a meaningful opportunity.

So the way I look at it, you have to strike a balance between the quality of the opportunity and the timing. In other words, if it's a poor opportunity I wouldn't make an exception; however, if it's a good opportunity, I would consider making an exception."

Agreement Number One

What model do I go to now? Agreement! "Good point," I said. [**reinforce**] "If someone's going to invest a year in something, it ought to be worthwhile" [**expand**]

Explanation - Part One

Then, I went on to my explanation. "As you know, I'm in the field of MIS and there is so much change occurring with computer technology that it is very difficult to keep current with the state-of-the-art. In fact, many people say that we in academia need to really reach out to the business community through consulting and research because we cannot keep current by staying on campus."

The dean interrupted by saying, "With the increase in technology change in your field, it must be very frustrating trying to keep on top of it all. I'm in marketing, myself, and don't have to deal too much with the technology component."

Agreement Number Two

What did I say? "You're absolutely right, it can be frustrating. [**reinforce**] In fact, some of my colleagues say you have to re-earn your Ph.D. every three to five years if you want to really be current in this field." [**expand**] Note that the dean interrupted my explanation with agreement. (No problem.) After reinforcing and expanding, I went on to the second part of the explanation.

Explanation - Part One (continued)

"At any rate, proper use of the leave of absence option is an attractive way to have an immersed relationship with an organization, and I wanted to find out as much as I could about how it works so that I understand how to exercise the option. The reason I am particularly interested in the leave of absence policy and your application of the guideline is because I've been approached by a leading company in the oil exploration business here in downtown Houston. Currently, all of this company's computer processing is done by a local outsourcing company. Plans are now being developed to build a state-of-the-art in-house computer center with all of the latest equipment and software. This company is sparing no expense to build a first-class computing facility with top people from all over the country.

The transition, from having their data processed externally to the in-house computer center, occurs later this year. More decisions regarding the implementation of new computer technology will be made during the next year than most companies make in seven years. I was presented with a very attractive opportunity to join the firm's management team as a key player in the planning and transition to the new computer center. [**problem**] The only way I could work with them would be to take a leave of absence. Are you open to that?" [**solution**]

The Dean's Response

Now the dean knows what's up. "Oh, Jim," he replied. "This is a problem for next year. We need you to cover classes."

Question/Confusion/Conflict

"So, your concern is who would teach my classes if I were on a leave of absence?" I asked. [**rephrase**]
"Yes, that's right!" he responded.

Realizing that the dean viewed this as conflict, I continued with, "Well, my schedule for next year includes a day-time undergraduate class and two evening graduate classes. One evening class is conducted on Mondays and Wednesdays and the other on Tuesdays and Thursdays. The company agreed that I can teach the evening classes, so there won't be a problem there. The only issue is the day-time undergraduate class, which can be covered by one of our Ph.D. students." **[minimize]**

Notice that I just agreed to work all day and teach four nights a week, to which you might react facetiously, 'Yeah, great communication skills! Now look at your situation!' However, I knew that the only way I could effectively minimize his conflict was to offer an alternative for covering the classes. (Would taking on this kind of work load be worth it to me? Yes!)

Dean's Response

"Well, that would work," he responded approvingly. "Downtown is close to the campus and we do have the Ph.D. students."

Agreement Number Three

"True," I said. **[reinforce]** "Since Ph.D. students are required to teach anyway, why not get one of them started right away?" **[expand]**

Probe Number Five

"Any other thoughts on this?" I asked. (Note: at this point I'm ready to close, so I'm checking to see if there are other concerns. Unfortunately, there are.)

The Dean's Response

"I am a little concerned about setting a precedence. Nobody has ever asked for a leave of absence after being here only one year. Although it is usually my decision, this could raise some eyebrows in the president's office and among the faculty."

Reservation/Doubt

Well, you wouldn't want to make an exception unless it was warranted and justified," I said. **[reassure]**

"That's right!" the dean emphasized.

I continued with, "Do you think it would be helpful to emphasize what the president has said and published about developing a stronger bond between academia and the real world? Might an opportunity like this be consistent with his thinking about our university reaching out to the business community? What better way to reach out to the business community than to loan them a faculty member at a critical time?" **[substantiate]**

The Dean's Response

"Good points, Jim!" he replied positively. "I think this leave of absence can easily be justified with a very positive twist."

Agreement Number Four

"You're right," I responded. **[reinforce]** "This really is a win-win situation for the university and the company." **[expand]**

Probe Number Six

"Any other thoughts?" I asked. (Note: I'm ready to close and I am wishing that he is also.)

The Dean's Response

At this point I started noticing some negative body language. The dean started stroking his eyebrow, then his ear (possible indication of doubt). After a short pause he said, "I'm just not sure about this, Jim."

Probe Number Seven

"Oh?" I said. **[indirect probe]**

The Dean's Response

"I'm concerned that you may not have really given academia a fair chance. I recall during your interview that you made the comment that you were not certain if you wanted to be a professor for the long term. You may well get lured back into the business world and decide not to return to the university."

Reservation/Doubt

(Note: Something I said when I interviewed for the faculty position was coming back to haunt me. During the interview the dean had pressed me on my ability to publish. I told him I would give it my best effort, but publishing was new to me and I couldn't make any guarantee. I further promised that if I could not deliver to the satisfaction of the university, I would return to industry where I knew I could be successful. At this point, whether or not I could publish was no longer a concern, since I had already published two books and several articles during my first year as a faculty member.)

Here is how I responded. "Well, it would not be in your or my best interest to grant me a leave of absence without resolving my commitment. **[reassure]** I can tell you that after being on the faculty for a full year, I am convinced that I made the right career choice and want to stay in academia for the long term. I have published 2 books and several articles already, and I really enjoy teaching. Also, please consider this, why would I agree to continue teaching my classes if I were not planning to return? You see, the reason I want to teach those classes is to assure you that I will be back." **[substantiate]**

The Dean's Response

The dean responded with, "I appreciate that, Jim—I'm convinced you'll return." Then he surprised me by saying, "Teaching two evening classes is too much. Why don't you just teach one class?" (That's the mirroring effect discussed in Chapter 3.)

Agreement Number Five

At this point, I knew it was a done deal, but I didn't want to take anything for granted. I replied, "That's very thoughtful of you. **[reinforce]** My concern is the graduate students might feel they are being cheated, so I don't mind teaching both classes. Also, by teaching both classes, no one on the faculty can take a cheap shot because you authorized my leave of absence." **[expand]**

The Dean's Response

"That sounds fine, Jim. Consider your request approved!"

Probe Number Eight

"Thank you very much," I replied. "Anything else?"

The Dean's Response

"No, nothing else at the moment," the dean replied.

Closure

(Now, *whew*, I was ready for a close!) "All right then, since this is an exceptional opportunity to work with the business community, consistent with the president's outreach program, and all of my classes are covered through my availability in the evenings and assigning a Ph.D. student for the day-time undergraduate class [**review points of agreement**], may I prepare an application for a leave of absence for your approval?" [**propose   course of action**]

The Dean's Response

"Sure, go ahead," the dean responded.

Unbelievable!

I was in his office for approximately 15 minutes. For two weeks afterward, there were people who would not believe I had gotten his approval. They kept saying, "No way! Not with only a year of experience on the faculty." But, my request was approved, and I had a great learning experience working for the oil company the following year.

It Only Works Most of the Time

When reflecting on my communication with the dean, I realized nothing significant happened in our conversation that I had not anticipated. Therein lies the power of using the models to analyze and prepare for important meetings or communication events. I spent hours thinking of all the issues that might come up to determine the best way to handle each of them.

I'm not saying that you will *get your way* all the time, but you accomplish more when you use the communication models. There are many other examples I could share with you. I selected this one because it was one of the most significant communication events in my career.

But, What If?

Occasionally, students in the Interpersonal Skills Seminar ask, "What would you have done had you been asked the purpose of the meeting when you called to schedule it?" I would have said, "I need to meet with the dean for personal reasons."

Another question students ask is, "Some people want you to get to your point right away. How do you know you'll be given the time to develop your explanation?" You try to make the time by thinking through in advance those questions and comments that develop a logical progression of thought. Your explanation should not be lengthy. However, it must be well constructed. The dean would not have wanted me to come into his office and say, "Listen, I've got a great opportunity to work with a company for a year. Can I have a leave of absence?" Everyone had already told me that he would say, "No", and I believe he would have, had I not communicated effectively and convincingly.

Do you like to say "no" when someone asks you for something? I really dislike having people in airports approach me and ask for a donation. I don't like saying "no" to them and I feel awkward ignoring them. I just wish they wouldn't ask. People generally don't like being asked questions that they have to answer with "No." I never would have put the dean in that position. The key is to ask the right

139

questions up front to find out whether you should make the request.

In the case study just presented, understand this was an important, significant professional request that I felt deserved 15 minutes of the dean's time. I took about two minutes asking a few quick questions to set the stage. Not a problem! What does matter is how the questions are asked. Avoid using an interrogative style because you may make the other person feel like he or she is being *set up*.

For example, what if I had gone into the dean's office and said, "I want to know three things. First of all, what is your policy on a leave of absence? Second, what exceptions have been made in the past? And, third, how do you feel about making exceptions?" Would such an approach have sounded like I was setting up a trap or trying to pin him in a corner? Ask your questions with the intent of wanting to learn more or better understand to create win-win situations. Then proceed with the other communication models.

Remember, even though the meeting I had with the dean took only 15 minutes, I invested several hours in preparation. It was well worth it!

Epilogue

By the way, the dean was a great guy. He asked me to be an associate dean and helped me get an early promotion from assistant professor to associate professor when I returned from the leave of absence.

The Rest of the Story

One aspect of this experience I would like to share with you is how I was able to ensure that I would have my evenings free to teach the two graduate classes. My first intention when approached by the oil exploration company was to work with them as a consultant rather than as a full-time employee. However, I wasn't sure if that would be acceptable.

So rather than making a statement such as, "The challenge sounds very interesting, but I could only work with you on a consulting basis," and having them respond with, "No, we're really only interested in people who can join us as full-time employees," I asked, "The challenge sounds very interesting, would you consider using me as a consultant during the transition period?"

Their response was the same, "No, we're only interested in people who can join us as full-time employees." Since I had asked a question rather than making a statement, I was able to continue with, "The university is just beginning its graduate degree program in MIS. As one of only two qualified professors in that field at the university, I could not, in good conscience, leave them stranded. I am scheduled to teach one day-time undergraduate class and two evening graduate classes. Since both of my graduate classes are conducted in the evenings, I may be able to pursue some arrangement with the university to allow me to work full-time during the day by using a Ph.D. student to teach my undergraduate class. I know that this company is in for a lot of challenges during the coming year and I may be able to contribute to meeting those challenges providing I can meet my teaching commitments. Do you think it will be possible for me to leave at 5:00 p.m. on Mondays through Thursdays to conduct my classes?"

I was assured that I could leave at 5:00 p.m. on the days that I had classes, and with that assurance, I could ensure the dean that I would be available to teach.

Knowing the communication models, understanding which one(s) to anticipate, and organizing the information before the meeting gave me the confidence to make such an incredible request.

14

Case Study: The Million-Dollar-An-Hour Conversation

As a second and insightful complete illustration of the use of the communication models in a critical situation, our next example is what Jim Wetherbe's colleagues in academia refer to as *the million-dollar-an-hour conversation.*

The context of this communication exercise was a one hour meeting with Fred Smith, CEO and founder of Federal Express Corporation, now renamed FedEx, headquartered in Memphis, Tennessee. My communication goal was to obtain a commitment for one million dollars in funding for creating a research center, to be named the FedEx Center for Cycle Time Research, at the University of Memphis.

FedEx Professorship

First, let me explain the concept of an endowed chair or professorship as it developed between the University of Memphis and FedEx. Information technology has always been a key part of the success of FedEx. Their tracking systems for packages and providing customer workstations for preparation of shipping and receiving of packages are well-known in the industry and frequently portrayed in their clever and innovative advertisements on television. Due to their strong interest in information technology, FedEx decided they wanted to attract a strong researcher in the field of information technology to the University of Memphis. To attract a professor for this role, FedEx worked with the University of Memphis and the state of Tennessee to establish an endowed chair.

An endowed chair is a position supported by a large endowment—in this case, two-and-one-half million dollars of combined state and FedEx money—and is one of the most prestigious achievements for a professor. The endowment money is invested and used to provide additional income and research support for the individual filling the endowed chair or professorship. In 1993, the University of Memphis offered me the distinct privilege of being the first holder of the FedEx Chair of Excellence in Information Technology.

FedEx Center for Cycle Time Research

As honored as I was to be offered the chair, I really was not interested in just *filling the chair* and *being scholarly* at the Fogelman College of Business at the University of Memphis. Rather, my objective was to establish a meaningful research relationship with FedEx. Dr. Lane Rawlins, the new president of the University of Memphis, was also very interested in enhancing the quality and prestige of the University of Memphis. Since FedEx was much more visible both nationally and internationally than the University of Memphis, my goal was to establish a relationship with FedEx through creation of a research program. This program could enhance visibility for the University, add value to FedEx, and provide a ground-breaking, strategic alliance for collaboration between universities and corporations working together.

To make this happen, I felt I needed to initiate a research program that would resonate with the people at FedEx and also be a viable research program for the University of Memphis. After contemplating this for a couple of months while I was interviewing for the FedEx chair position, I conceived the idea for a center for *cycle time research*.

The purpose of the center would be to conduct research on ways to reduce the time required for completing organizational processes while also reducing cost and increasing customer service. Organizational processes include activities such as processing insurance claims, admitting patients to a hospital, designing a product, establishing credit, scheduling a class, ordering a product, or moving a package from point A to point B. Comprised of a selected group of faculty, FedEx staff, and students, the FedEx Center for Cycle Time Research would be dedicated to:

1. Performing research projects that address cycle time reduction issues
2. Developing and documenting the innovations to reduce cycle time
3. Providing benchmark cycle times on various business processes

The results of the research program would be disseminated through seminars and *Cycle Time Research*, a newly created journal.

The idea for the *FedEx Center for Cycle Time Research* went over well at the University of Memphis—from the President's office to the Provost's office to the Dean's office and to my immediate colleagues (all of which, of course, involved several critical communication exercises). The problem was that we needed a grant to create such a center. Obtaining such a grant involved setting up a meeting with FedEx management, preferably with Fred Smith the CEO and founder, to explore whether FedEx would be interested in supporting the center. We hoped they would view such a center to be supportive of FedEx's goal of reducing cycle time for its customers in all aspects of their business logistics—not just in shipping packages.

I requested Dr. Rawlins to contact Fred Smith and ask for an hour of his time to meet with me as the candidate the University was recruiting for the FedEx professorship. Mr. Smith graciously agreed.

Walking in Memphis—in Fred Smith's Shoes

Realizing I would have only one hour to make my point, I knew I had to invest substantial *upfront* time to make the best use of that one important hour. So I began reading every book and article I could find to understand more about FedEx, it's management, and particularly Fred Smith. I talked with people who currently and previously worked at FedEx and tried to understand the rationale that would be most conducive to a positive decision to support the Center for Cycle Time Research. Overall, I spent about 80 hours in preparation—which turned out to be an incredibly good use of my time based on the very beneficial things I learned.

I knew before I started that understanding Fred Smith was critical to making this communication exercise a success. My research provided many insights into this incredible entrepreneur. I also discovered through my reading that contrary to some people in such positions who have very strong egos and are primarily interested in enhancing their reputations, Fred Smith is definitely not an egomaniac. Rather, he is very modest, even self-effacing. Like many of the greatest leaders, he is an humble person. Fred Smith is incredibly focused on continuing to make FedEx a better and more successful corporation. His efforts are not for self-glory. (An obvious conclusion from this insight is not to propose naming the FedEx Center the Fred Smith Center for Cycle Time Research!) He feels an enormous loyalty to the people working in his organization. In fact, one of the things FedEx is known for is its *no lay-off* policy—an incredible accomplishment given the economic conditions facing organizations in the 1980s and 1990s.

I also learned Fred Smith is an avid reader and very much a scholar in his own right. This made me optimistic that he might be inclined to support an intellectual pursuit such as a research program in cycle time reduction. Fred is also a risk taker. Besides founding one of the most successful companies of the past three decades, he initiated the largest venture capital start-up in the history of the world when creating FedEx. Ironically, the concept of FedEx was based upon a paper Fred Smith authored while a student at Yale University—for which he received a grade of C from his economics professor. Obviously, Fred Smith is <u>not</u> easily discouraged. Fred is also a hometown boy who has done well and continues to *do good*—an icon within Memphis and a strong supporter of the community.

If Fred Smith were to agree to support this Center, he would have to view it as a truly productive and helpful research program that would contribute to FedEx and its customers. In other words, it would have to be a *value added* operation. Regardless of his reputation for supporting the community and the University, Fred Smith would not likely give the money just for the recognition of supporting the university or for enhancing his visibility.

Issues To Absolutely, Positively Be Prepared For

As I was preparing for what might occur in proposing a Center for Cycle Time Research, there were two key issues that I felt would *absolutely, positively* have to be dealt with to achieve a successful result:

1. More money already?
2. How can I be sure it's a good investment?

Question/Confusion/Conflict

One possible problem area was that having provided part of the funding for the endowed chair, Fred could raise the fair and legitimate question, "We gave money for the endowment, why are we being asked to give again?"

Therefore in preparing for this issue, I had logically built on FedEx's previous contribution where the intent of the endowment was to attract a person committed to doing high quality research in the area of information technology at the University of Memphis. That, in fact, was being accomplished. While showing appreciation for FedEx's prior generosity, the approach in requesting a million dollars to establish the center was that we were not asking for a gift, but rather a contract to do research. I knew I would have to convey how the Center could do research beneficial to FedEx for

147

less cost and greater value than FedEx could do it. Research skills are a core competency of faculty; plus, through the use of Ph.D. students, research can be produced much less expensively. The bottom line was that the Center could return at least two to three million dollars in value for the one million dollars we were asking FedEx to invest in research.

The key point had to be that FedEx was making an investment for which they would receive a return. This was <u>not a gift</u>.

Reservation/Doubt

The other major issue which I thought I would have to be prepared to handle was any reservations or doubts Fred Smith might have about the Center's ability to deliver high quality research. My planned substantiation for this issue was to reference my 15-year track record of directing the Management Information Systems Research Center (MISRC) at the University of Minnesota. The MISRC has had twenty-five (25) corporate sponsors over the years. I would provide Fred Smith with the names of key people in those sponsoring companies in the Twin Cities that he could contact to ask if they felt the money invested in research programs under my direction delivered much more value than they cost.

An Hour with a Legend

Fred Smith turned out to be everything I had been told he was —warm, a gentleman, incredibly bright, and well-read. In a very short time, I was aware that Fred had done his homework as well. He knew much about my background and track record, books and articles that I had written, and was very generous with his compliments about my previous work. (Can you imagine the honor of having a person of Fred Smith's stature check out a professor's background?)

As our conversation progressed beyond the initial cordial, get-acquainted topics, I had the opportunity to use these two explanation models:

Explanation Model 1

"There is a problem with higher education in this country—it's out of touch and not delivering what the market expects—which is reflected in the amount of funding available. As you know from your business, the market doesn't lie to you. If the market isn't providing you with resources, you probably are not meeting its needs. The University of Memphis is no exception. Resources are very limited there. [**problem**]

I would like to share with you some ideas for trying to address these problems in a win-win way. We have a unique opportunity to demonstrate how a university and a corporation can work together to establish an alliance around a research program which is meaningful, adds value, and is worthy of being funded.

A key operational component at FedEx is reducing cycle time as a value added part of your relationships with your customers. What I would like to explore with you is creating a research center to advance and disseminate knowledge revolving around reducing cycle time of business processes. The research that we would do could be both internal to FedEx, that is, reducing cycle time within FedEx—one of your major agendas; and external for your customers as a value-added service helping them reduce their cycle time. This could further improve the partnership relationship that you cultivate with your customers." [**solution**]

Fred was interested and asked me to continue.

Explanation Model 2

"Organizations in all industries are under increasing pressure to get more done with fewer resources to remain competitive. A key concept in achieving this is reducing cycle time. By reducing cycle time, organizations can reduce cost or opportunity cost, increase quality, and improve customer service. All too often in organizations, less than 3% of the elapsed time involved in performing a process has anything to do with real work. The rest of the time is spent on scheduling, waiting, needless repetition, getting lost, getting found, expediting; in other words, *the left hand not knowing what the right hand is doing.* For example, it might take a month to process an insurance claim in elapsed time but only 15 minutes in actual *work* time. [**problem**]

By making innovative use of information technology, operations management, empowerment, behavior modification, organizational redesign, outsourcing, parallel processing, economic analysis, etc., we can reengineer business processes to eliminate waste and nonsense—thereby cost-effectively reducing cycle time. We could jointly offer much value to organizations world-wide by creating a center focused on developing strategies and methods for reducing cycle time, shared through journals and seminars." [**solution**]

(Wonderfully, this was one of those days when everything was going right. I have found that when I am well-prepared, objections or doubts are infrequent). Fred liked the idea—and asked how much funding we needed. I responded, "One million dollars to be spread over a three-year period." (Gulp, the cards had been dealt.)

Fred said he would like to support the Center, but never makes such decisions without consulting his senior executives. He asked me to put together a written proposal for him to present the idea to FedEx management. He also affirmed that he was aware I needed fast cycle time in their response, so I could make my decision to accept or not accept the professorship. Fred committed that within one week of receiving my written proposal, he and his management team would make a decision *to go* or *not go* with the one million dollar grant.

I thanked Fred for his time, reiterating what I had mentioned earlier in the conversation, and that I was leaving his office to catch a flight to Europe. I would be gone for a week, but that I would get the proposal to him as quickly as I could.

Uh-Oh—This is a Test!

As I was riding in the taxi to the Memphis airport to catch the first leg of my flight to Berlin that Friday afternoon, I was thinking, 'It's too bad I can't get this proposal to him until I get back from Europe. Then it struck me—I was being tested! I had just espoused the value of getting things done quickly to Fred Smith. He indicated he could make a million dollar decision within a week after receiving my proposal, but then I had implied I could not get a proposal to him until I got back from Europe.'

One of the great stereotypes about academic personnel is that they tend not to be goal or results-oriented, and the old stigma, *"those who can do, those who can't do, teach"* continues. I had to find a way to get this proposal to Fred—*fast!*

When I arrived at the Memphis airport, I called and asked a colleague to meet me with a laptop computer at the airport in Boston where I was connecting for my international flight. Then I wrote the proposal on the flight to Boston. During the one-and-one-half hour layover in Boston, we converted my handwritten notes to a digital version of the proposal. My colleague agreed to transmit the proposal to Fred Smith's office on Monday morning. I had to prove that I practiced what I preached.

Epilogue

Well, as you might have guessed by now, I accepted the professorship, and Fred Smith and his management team agreed to support the FedEx Center for Cycle Time Research. It was founded in the fall of 1993. The first issue of *Cycle Time Research* was published in January of 1994. Having the opportunity to create the Center for Cycle Time Research and work with the incredible people at FedEx has been one of the most rewarding aspects of my career.

The following two quotes from the FedEx Center for Cycle Time Research brochure illustrate the commitment between FedEx and the University of Memphis in establishing their research alliance:

Investing in cycle time research is vital to the future of FedEx. To remain competitive in today's global economy, companies must relentlessly pursue innovations that speed the flow on information as well as their products and services. The benefits we'll gain from research carried out at the Center for Cycle Time Research will far exceed our investment and will prove invaluable not just to FedEx, but to all companies.

Fred W. Smith, CEO of FedEx

The FedEx Center is an opportunity for the University of Memphis to work in partnership with major American business and a perfect example of what a major university should be doing.

V. Lane Rawlins,
President of The University of Memphis

The final tribute to the results of their relationship is the following letter from Fred Smith to the President of the University of Memphis:

January 20, 1995

President V. Lane Rawlins
The University of Memphis
Office of the President
Memphis, TN 38152

Dear Dr. Rawlins:

I wanted to let you know how pleased we are with the Cycle Time Research partnership between FedEx and the University of Memphis. Jim Wetherbe provided the executive seminar and copies of the Cycle Time Research journal at the FedEx Orange Bowl in Miami. We have key customer executives from around the world attend this seminar. The response was extremely positive. Several participants indicated it was the best seminar they had ever attended. There was also lots of interest from companies to participate in future cycle time research projects.

The research team at the University of Memphis is doing a great job of researching real world problems in a pragmatic manner. The new journal and Jim's seminar are straightforward and quite accessible to a business community. We plan to distribute the journal to key executives worldwide.

The original vision of a meaningful, win-win working relationship between FedEx and the University of Memphis is definitely coming to fruition. The FedEx Center is promoting both FedEx and the University of Memphis while creating a powerful and useful core competency in cycle time. We at FedEx are very satisfied with the results of our investment.

Sincerely,

Fred W. Smith
CEO, FedEx

Summary

This particular communication exercise obviously represents one of the most important in my career. Knowing the communication models, understanding which ones to anticipate, and organizing the information before the meeting gave me the confidence to make such an incredible request. And, although I did not have to deal with questions/confusion/conflict or reservation/doubt in this instance, I certainly would not have wanted to go *walking in Memphis* without having *the map* of the communication models and being prepared. Otherwise, this could have been one of the most humiliating hours of my career.

By the way, guess how many of my friends and colleagues thought I had a chance of getting a million dollar commitment from a one hour meeting? Less than five percent—the rest thought I had a better chance for an Elvis sighting!

Making the Models Work for You

Knowing the steps to take is one thing, but it is quite another to develop the skill to take those steps. The next chapter, *Practicing the Models*, offers some practical ways for you to develop and improve your skill in using the verbal and non-verbal communication skills presented in this book.

> *By using the communication models, you can simulate*
> *and rehearse, through role playing, about 95 percent*
> *of what will occur during a meeting or event.*

15

Practicing the Models

Do you recall when the United States first put a man on the moon. That remarkable event has been replayed many times on television. If you have ever seen the documentary on the lunar landing you may remember hearing the same response in answer to the question from ground control, "How are things going?" Throughout the entire process, the flight commander responded, "Great, just like we rehearsed it." What did he mean? The three astronauts who prepared for that adventure practiced by simulating everything they thought they might encounter over and over— obviously, there was little room for mistakes!

You can use that same strategy to simulate meetings and other important communication events. By using the communication models, you can simulate and rehearse, through role playing, about 95 percent of what will occur during a meeting or event.

How Ronald Reagan Beat Father Time

Remember the second television debate between Ronald Reagan and Walter Mondale when they were campaigning for president in the 1980s? Do you recall why Reagan won that debate? Many analysts think it was because of the age issue. During the debate a question about Reagan's age was presented by one of the debate panelists. Reagan smiled and laughed a little and said, "Now, I'm not going to let age be a factor in this campaign or this debate. The fact that my opponent is younger and less-experienced than I am should not be an issue." He got everyone to laugh and diffused any attack on his age. Do you think Reagan's response was simulated and rehearsed? You better believe it was! That response was not spontaneous.

Practice Makes Perfect

To really become proficient in using the communication models takes drill and practice, and more drill and more practice. You use the same approach as you would to master the fundamentals of a sport, learn to play a musical instrument, or become fluent in a foreign language.

Figure 15.1 is an outline showing all six of the verbal communication models and related processes. This can be useful in helping you picture the important aspects of the models as a group.

Let Your Memory Serve You

Try to memorize the processes related to each of the six verbal communication models. Once you have learned **What** to do in each circumstance you can more easily focus on learning **How** to master the process of communicating effectively. At this point, you can actually develop a script for each model based on the *John working overtime* theme used throughout this book or based on a situation that is meaningful to you. Taking the time to actually develop content and write down a script for each process of every model is a great technique to help you internalize these communication skills.

In addition, a script provides a tool for practicing. Here's how to practice. Find someone to role play with you using the script you have written—preferably someone who has also read this book. Present your problem and solution explanation.

Your role-playing partner then picks any response he or she wishes from the script, and your challenge is to deal with it according to the appropriate model. The diagram in Figure 15.2 can serve as a guide to help you categorize responses and visualize the communication flow as the communication process unfolds.

QUERY
Indirect Probe
Direct Probe

EXPLANATION
Problem
Solution

AGREEMENT
Reinforce
Expand

RESERVATION/DOUBT
Reassure
Substantiate

QUESTION/CONFUSION/CONFLICT
Rephrase
Answer/Clarify/Minimize

CLOSURE
Review Points of Agreement
Propose Course of Action

Figure 15.1 VERBAL COMMUNICATION MODELS

You can think of Figure 15.2 as a *map* of the communication models to navigate through conversations similar to using a GPS. The six models allow you to know your exact location in a conversation and the direction needed to achieve the desired outcome.

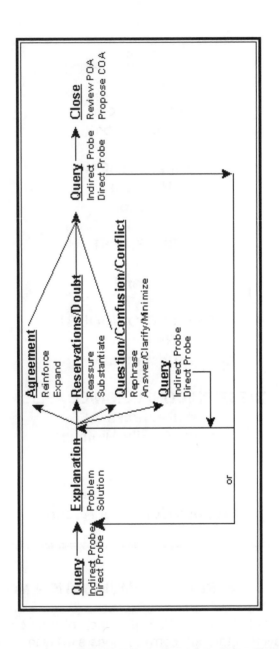

Figure 15.2 COMMUNICATION FLOW DIAGRAM

One More Time, John Works Overtime

We are going to have John work overtime one more time. As the dialogue unfolds, see if you can follow along by mapping it against Figure 15.2. Notice as in Figure 15.2, the conversation starts with a query rather than going directly to an explanation.

Your query: Good afternoon. Have you got a couple of minutes?

Response: Sure, what's on your mind?

Your query: Have you heard about the situation with payroll processing?

Response: No, I haven't. Tell me more.

Your explanation: Well, the payroll transactions came in late today. As a result, there is not enough time left in the day to process them for distribution on Monday. What do you think of having John work overtime this week to get the payroll transactions processed so people can get paid on Monday? (Note that rather than *stating*, "I think John should work overtime...," you *asked*, "What do you think of...")

Response: No way! I'm not covering for payroll. It's their problem!

Your rephrase: So, you're saying that since the payroll department made the mistake, it's not our problem?

Response: Yes, that's right.

Your minimization: It certainly is the payroll department's mistake. However, one thing you may want to consider is how people may react on Monday when they don't get their paychecks. Will we get in trouble because we could have saved the day, but didn't just to make a point to payroll? Do you think that might create any problems for us?

Response: Well, it might. You've made a good point, but I'm not convinced it's absolutely necessary to have John work overtime. Don't we have any other alternatives?

Your reassurance and substantiation: We certainly don't want to ask someone to work overtime unless it's absolutely necessary. Here is what we are up against. It takes eight full hours to process the payroll transactions. We have only one hour left in the work day. Even if we put our two available people on it, there is just not enough time left. We really are in an overtime situation.

Response: I guess you're right, but the problem is we just don't have any funds left in the budget for over time.

Your rephrase: Oh, so your concern is the lack of money budgeted for overtime?

Response: Yes, that's right.

Your minimization: Good news. I've discussed the situation with the payroll manager, and he has agreed to pay for any overtime required to get the transactions processed out of his budget.

Response: How does John feel about working overtime this weekend? Any problems there?

Your rephrase:	You are concerned about John's availability?
Response:	Yes, it may upset him to have to work overtime.
Your answer:	I checked with him and he told me he would be glad to work this weekend so he could earn some extra money for his vacation.
Response:	Great! Let's do it then.
Your query:	OK, I'll get things rolling. Anything else?
Response:	No, that's all for now.
Your review & proposal:	Good. So, since we need to get the payroll transactions processed and the payroll department has agreed to pay for overtime and John has agreed to work the overtime, I'll go ahead and get the schedule set up. Is that all right?
Response:	Sounds good to me. Thanks!

That is how to practice with a script of responses that your role-playing partner can use. The idea is for the responses to vary at random while you deal with each one according to the appropriate model. You can develop several scripts to work with until you have internalized how to use the models almost effortlessly. The key is recognizing what's *coming over the communication net* and dealing with it accordingly.

To help you document your practice scripts, there are several blank pages in the back of the book along with another picture of the Communication Flow Diagram shown as Figure 15.2 for you to cut out and use as a handy reference when first practicing and learning the verbal communication models.

Use High-Stress, Inconsequential Situations

Another way that you can practice using these models is in high-stress, inconsequential situations. Some examples include when you are returning merchandise and the store clerk is giving you a hassle or when you are receiving poor service in a restaurant and want to improve the situation without creating an argument.

Starving In Denver

We have pointed out the power of the probe many times in this book. One of the best probes to use is the question of fairness.

I was on a coast-to-coast flight some time ago and had a short layover in Denver. Because the catering service had forgotten to heat the food prior to loading, no food on the flight leading into Denver had been heated. All of the dinners were still frozen.

I got off the airplane for the few minutes we were allowed and started looking for anything that resembled food. I found a hot dog stand and said, "I'll have a hot dog and a diet coke."

The attendant replied, "I don't have any hot dogs, I ran out."

I could see hot dog buns stacked to the ceiling, so I said, "Fine, I'll take two hot dog buns and a Diet Coke."

"OK," the guy said as he gave me the Coke, "But I'll have to charge you the price of two hot dogs."

Now, I treat that as conflict! I asked in a kind, disbelieving voice, "You mean to tell me that you are going to give me two buns without any meat and charge me the same price as if they had meat?" (That rephrase by itself would make you uncomfortable, wouldn't it?)

He reluctantly said, "Yeah, those are the rules."

I gave him my widest and most sincere puppy-dog eyes and said, "Do you think that's fair?"

He paused for a moment and then, looking rather embarrassed, said, "Here, just take them and go."

The fairness question usually works, but not always. Sometimes people will give you this response: "No, it's not fair, but then life is not fair." An effective question to ask is, "That's true, but does it matter to you personally whether or not you are fair?"

Are You Using Enough Probes?

I have generally gotten myself into communication problems as a result of not asking enough questions. For example, I was checking out of a hotel where I was conducting a seminar. It was the last day of a five-day seminar, and I was running late because I had not received my wake-up call.

Once I was dressed, I went to the check-out counter and asked, "What is the latest time I can check out today?" The attendant said, "Twelve noon." I asked, "Do you have any flexibility on that?" "No, we don't," was the response. "Well, here's the problem," I said. "I'm conducting a seminar here at the hotel. I left a wake-up call, but nobody called me this morning. I woke up with just enough time to get dressed. The seminar is not over until 12:30, and then I have to attend a luncheon. I really can't get back in time to get packed and checked out before noon. **[problem]** Can you make an exception for me?" **[solution]**

The attendant said, "Let me check to see what happened to your wake-up call." After a short time he said, "Our records show that you put in a request for a wake-up call at 10:30 last night, and it was canceled at 3:00 a.m. this morning. Our policy is to hold firm on the 12:00 noon check-out time so the housecleaning service has enough time to get all of the rooms cleaned before 4:00 p.m." (I found out later that several of the seminar participants had decided to stay out late and thought it would be helpful if I slept in too, so one of them canceled my wake-up call—great practical joke!)

Here was my mistake. I had already accused the hotel of not giving me a wake-up call. The attendant denied my request to delay my check-out time and became defensive.

What should I have said? "I scheduled a wake-up call at 10:30 last night. Is there any reason why I would not have gotten my wake-up call this morning?" [an additional probe before committing myself]. The attendant may have responded, "Let me check. I see that you scheduled a wake-up call; however, it was canceled at

3:00 a.m." I could have replied, "Well, I did not make that cancel-lation. How could that have happened?" Then the attendant prob-ably would say, "I guess anyone could have canceled your wake-up call. There could have been a mistake." By using probes I keep it a win-win situation.

The minute I made an accusation, the hotel staff became defensive. Generally, if you politely ask enough questions you can get a satisfactory resolution.

What Are Content-Rich Questions?

Occasionally during our Interpersonal Skills Seminar, someone says, "It seems to me that if I ask questions so much of the time rather than making statements, people might start to think I don't know anything!" Not if you influence their thinking by the types of questions you ask. You see, there are content-free questions and there are content-rich questions.

Here is an example of a content-free question: "So, what do you want to do?" A content-rich question would be, "What do you think about enhancing all our web sites with video streaming tech-nology?" When you ask content-rich questions and concurrently send a non-verbal message of confidence, you won't have to worry that other people might think you don't know anything because you ask questions.

What About Meetings?

Another issue that frequently comes up is the use of communi-cation models during meetings. You can use basically the same techniques and body language for a group that you would with an individual. You may have to make some adjustments if you are standing while the remainder of the group is sitting down, or if you are sitting at the head of a conference table and some attendees are seated where it is difficult to see them. When someone asks a question, rephrase and answer it, then continue the meeting. If your boss is in the room you might want to keep an eye on his or her body language to get a sense of comfort level. If someone asks you a question about a sensitive issue you feel you are not qualified to answer, you might refer that question to your boss.

Power to the People

Almost every time we conduct the Interpersonal Skills Seminar, someone makes the comment, "These techniques are very powerful. It appears as though a person could really manipulate other people by using them. Is that a problem?" The response to that question really depends upon your definition of manipulation. In the area of interpersonal relationships, you manipulate other people by being shrewd and devious to profit at their expense or to their detriment. Frankly, you can use the techniques discussed in this book for those purposes quite effectively.

Remember, however, the whole purpose of learning these techniques and developing your communication skills is to become a more effective communicator. Part of the process is learning to see and understand another person's point of view. You do that through probing, listening, reinforcing, reassuring, rephrasing, and reviewing. Understanding other people's perspectives so you can address their concerns, manage their expectations, overcome objections, and avoid misunderstandings is mutually beneficial, not manipulative. Communicating effectively results in win-win situations.

The Joy of Teaching

One of the rewarding aspects of teaching these seminars on interpersonal skills is seeing participants use the class as a forum to solve a current problem they are facing. They often take what they learn in class and apply it to a *real-world* situation. When they share the results of their efforts with the class, they vividly demonstrate the value of practice and the power of the communication models.

Role playing is really where an understanding of how to use the communication models comes alive. And, role playing is also where one begins to really understand the importance of applying drill and practice to learn the skills required to master these communication techniques. The role playing in a classroom environment ranges from dealing with teenage children, to interaction with spouses, to work-related situations. The situation can vary from a discussion about staying out late, in the case of a teenager, to major confrontations between senior business executives.

Case in Point

The following brief illustration demonstrates how effective communication can turn frustration into joy and satisfaction. Bond Wetherbe, co-author of this book, recently conducted a session on interpersonal skills as part of a year-long certification program for managers of medical and dental practices. He tells how one of his students put learning into action.

Part of the training in verbal communication skills includes role playing between the students and me. Each student chooses a topic for explanation and we build on that as we discuss each of the six communication models. We encourage the students to pick real-world situations in the workplace, home, or other settings where they have interpersonal relationships.

Putting the Models to Work

Sandra, the office manager at a medical practice, chose to use a work-related situation for her role playing. She had been trying for six months to get Linda, the office accountant and wife of the leading physician, to make a decision on purchasing a new copy machine. The old copy machine was obsolete and continually breaking down, requiring expensive and time-consuming repairs. It was a real point of frustration for the entire office staff.

Several months had gone by since Linda had requested that Sandra collect information on copy machine replacement alternatives. And still no decision had been made, even though Linda had been given the information almost immediately after her request. Every time Sandra would ask Linda if she had made a decision, Linda's response would be, "No, not yet, I have not had time to review the material." Sandra pleaded on behalf of the staff to Linda,"Please make a decision. This old copy machine is driving us nuts!"

During my role playing with Sandra about this problem, her frustration with the situation was very apparent. When I expressed reservation, doubt, or conflict when playing the role of Linda, she became very exasperated and reverted to argument. Finally, Sandra said, "Look, I'm really trying to learn how to use the models, but I've been fighting this situation for so long that I just don't know what to do. Can you help me develop an explanation that will get her to make a decision?" I said, "Sure, let's work on that."

By now, the whole class had become interested in her dilemma and were curious about what to do. I asked Sandra if she thought that the real problem was that Linda just could not make up her mind for one reason or another. Sandra said, "I hadn't thought about that; but no, I don't think that is the problem ."

"Based on your research to get her the information she requested and your knowledge of your office requirements, do you know the best alternative for a replacement machine?" I asked. "I sure do!" she replied. "Then why don't we build an explanation that proposes having you make the procurement decision as the solution?" I said. Sandra looked doubtful and said, "Well, I don't know if that will work. Linda usually makes those decisions. She is the doctor's wife you know." I asked, "Would you be willing to make the decision on what copy machine to buy if Linda gave you the OK?" "Yes I would," Sandra replied. "Let's go for it!"

I won't go into the entire script here; however, the explanation went something like this:

"Good morning Linda. Do you have a few minutes you can share with me?" (Assume a positive response from Linda.)

"As we have discussed previously, our old copy machine is no longer adequate for the office demands. Several months ago, you asked me do some research on some procurement alternatives and provide you with that information, which I did. I know how busy you are with all of the accounting for the office, and I'm sure you just haven't had the time to review the material I gave you. The staff has asked me to speak to you about their frustration, loss in productivity, and impact on morale caused by the copy machine continually breaking down. It spends more time awaiting repairs than in operation, and I'll bet you are tired of paying the repair bills.

After conducting the research you asked me to do, I did a comparative analysis to determine what machine would most effectively meet our office needs. If you feel comfortable with my judgment, would it be all right if I go ahead and prepare a purchase order for your signature to get a new copy machine?"

Three weeks later, I was teaching a different session for the same class members, having not seen them in the interim. Sandra came up to me just beaming and said, "It worked! It really worked!" And I said, not remembering, "What worked?" "The explanation we developed!" she said. "I have been trying for six months to get a new copy machine for my office, and after using these communication skills, I had it in three days!" She went on to say, "I still can't believe it, the whole office is really grateful."

Sandra told me how she practiced her explanation and thought through how she would respond, using the other models if necessary. As things turned out, she didn't have to use anything but Agreement and Closure. After her presentation of the problem, using a logical progression of thought along with an impact statement on an issue important to her listener, her solution was approved. Through her explanation of the problem and solution, Sandra created a situation that was mutually beneficial. She created a win-win situation.

The Models Work in Many Different Situations

Problems resulting from poor communicating techniques that have been solved through role playing in seminar classes cover a broad scope. They range from our example of getting a new copy machine, to convincing a boss that someone deserved a pay raise, to persuading a CEO to have his company acquired, and to something really difficult, convincing a child to go to bed at an early hour!

Perhaps the key insight gained through observing and experiencing role playing is knowing the communication models and what steps to take next are not enough! Acquiring the skill required to use this knowledge is really the crucial element that transforms knowledge into effective behavior. The key to acquiring that skill is drill and practice.

Back to the Fundamentals

We discussed the importance of learning the fundamentals of any activity at length at the beginning of this book. Many people make the mistake of thinking that just playing tennis, golf, or any other sport helps them become better. That is rarely true! What makes people become better at tennis or golf is 1) taking lessons from a professional instructor; and 2) drill and practice. In the case of tennis, that means returning thousands of balls with the forehand, thousands of balls with the backhand, and thousands of balls with the overhead smash. In the case of golf, it means practicing at the driving range with woods and long irons, at the practice green for chipping and pitching with short irons and wedges, and on the putting green with every golfer's most used club, the putter, over and over.

You now have the fundamentals for effective communication. Develop your own scripts and practice routines for becoming an expert at applying the appropriate communication *strokes*.

Spread the News

One interesting question that frequently comes up is, "If several people in an organization really learn to use these models well, could that cause problems, especially if they have to communicate with each other?" Absolutely not. We wish that everyone we interacted with knew how to use these communication models. People are much easier to interact with when they explain problems before presenting solutions, make sure they understand what may be bothering me before trying to deal with it, and provide alternative perspectives for something they anticipate I might not like.

These models really do make the communicating process much more effective than relying on knee-jerk reactions. But what if you have not done your homework?

You've Got to be Able to Adjust

Suppose that something comes up that you're not prepared for or haven't anticipated. In our original example, suppose John has in fact put in a lot of overtime in the past few weeks, and you haven't discussed his working this weekend with him. When questioned about John's availability for working overtime, you can say, "Why don't I check with John and see if he is available to work this weekend?" What you have done is changed or modified your objective for the meeting. Your original objective may have been to get approval for John to work overtime. Now you have to settle for finding out whether or not John is available to work overtime. Later you can get back to your boss to confirm the solution.

Remember in Chapter 10 where I discussed the use of spreadsheet software on PCs with Susan, the vice president of Finance, and I finally asked her, "What would it take to convince you?" I find out right then what the course of action is going to be. Once I complete that course of action, I can schedule another meeting.

It isn't always necessary to try to accomplish everything in one meeting. You may set out to accomplish more than you are able to in one meeting because someone doesn't believe you, wants more substantiation, or asks you to come up with different minimization alternatives. When someone can't make a decision after you have substantiated or minimized, ask, "Well, what would it take to convince you?" After he or she tells you what it would take, you can ask, "OK then, if I obtain the facts you need to convince you, will you be comfortable with this solution?" "Yes, I'll be comfortable," should be the response. Then you can close with, "We've agreed on several things today, A, B, and C, but we still need to resolve D and E, so my course of action is to get that information for you and then we'll meet again. Is that all right with you?"

Converting Knowledge to Power

Now that you have learned the fundamental techniques of communicating, you can analyze and understand the dynamics of any conversation or meeting. Through drill and practice you can master the application of these techniques. As you learn to use the models, take time to review their effectiveness, and critique yourself after important meetings and conversations. You now have the **knowledge to make your point**. Drill and practice develops the **skills** you need to *effectively and successfully* make your point.

PART FIVE

Expanding the Models

*Using a hook question gets their attention
while the social contract keeps their attention.*

16

Making Your Point & Scoring Points Through Presentation Skills

One of the questions frequently asked when conducting seminars or workshops on effective interpersonal communication is, "Can these models apply when speaking or presenting to a group of people?" The answer is an emphatic **yes**. In fact, by using both the verbal and non-verbal communication models, you can create a speech or presentation that engages your audience and at the same time helps you overcome the nervousness or fear that is often associated with speaking in front of a group of people.

Public Speaking

Do you know what the number one fear is of most people? You guessed it, public speaking! You may have heard the somewhat macabre eulogy example where people say "I would rather be the deceased, than be the person delivering the eulogy."

What about you? Is public speaking stressful to you? Does is make you feel self-conscious? Well, you are certainly not alone if you answered "yes". When I was in college many years ago, I absolutely dreaded having to get up in front of a class and give a presentation—say, a book report for example. I would be so nervous in front of the class that my voice would quiver and my knees would shake so badly that my pants legs looked like they were flapping in a strong breeze! I so disliked that speaking to a group of people made me so nervous that I vowed to find a way to overcome it. I read several books on public speaking, talked about it with people who did it well, but nothing seemed to help. Then, one day, while reading the Parade Magazine from the Sunday newspaper, I came across a short article asking about how the great past Prime Minister of England, Winston Churchill, became such an outstanding orator.

The answer was based on an interview with Winston Churchill where he was asked that very question and he responded that in his early years he had a lisp or stutter impairment that caused him to be quite self-conscious when speaking in public. He consistently worked to overcome his impairment and at one point realized that in the process of speaking publicly, the *focus should be on the audience and what is being said* rather than on him personally—and with that insight, he quickly overcame being nervous and self-conscious while speaking publicly. He later stated, "My impediment is no hindrance."

For some reason, that article really resonated with me, and I personally adopted the following steps when preparing for a presentation.

1. Focus on the audience members—they are important, not me.

2. Focus on content—what I want to communicate and having my listeners understand is what matters.

3. Present the content in a caring way using a logical progression of thought that helps my audience gain understanding—use a "teaching approach".

Applying these three steps enabled me to quickly overcome being stressed out about giving presentations as I completed college and moved into the work place. I encourage you to try the steps—make them work for you as well.

Observations on Public Speaking

Have you ever noticed the difference in a speaker who stands stiffly and formally behind a podium during the presentation and only at the end really engages the audience during the Question and Answer session? The difference can be like night and day! In the "formal" presentation, he or she may appear rather cold and indifferent but when the Q&A session begins, he or she moves from behind the podium, becomes more animated, warm and friendly—sometimes even smiling and laughing with the audience.

This frequently happens because during the Q&A session, the speaker's focus naturally shifts to the audience. The interaction becomes almost a one-on-one conversation with the person who asked the question—even though the answer is meant for everyone. If you've noticed, it seems like most of the value gained from the presentation occurs during this more relaxed Q&A session where there is two-way dialogue between the speaker and audience. Frequently, supportive comments and contributions come from audience members. Every one in the room seems to be in a more comfortable zone with ideas being exchanged and the learning process accelerating. As a professor, these are the times that are most rewarding and gratifying.

Getting in the Comfort Zone

What if we could actually start a presentation with a Q&A session, or at least simulate it initially, and invoke those *comfort zone* dynamics from the start? Well, we can do exactly that when we apply the communication models to the presentation process. If you recall in the Communication Flow Diagram, starting a conversation with a question, especially one that could lead to important outcomes, gives you an advantage. Chapter 10, **Query Model**, points out that the question is the single most powerful communication tool you can learn!

By using the Query Model to begin a presentation you engage your audience at the outset and create a more relaxed and interactive environment for your presentation. The added value of this approach is that it:

1. creates a one-on-one frame of mind;

2. focuses immediately on the message;

3. allows you to find out what your audience already knows.

Practical Aspects of Giving a Presentation

How do I Prepare?

Preparation for giving a presentation is very much like preparing for an important one-on-one conversation. If you recall in the Case Study Chapters, I presented several of the questions I was considering using to close friends and colleagues prior to the critical meetings, and asked for their opinions on what I might anticipate or expect in response. I also considered what they thought were key issues and included those in my preparation process.

The same approach applies to preparing for a presentation. The point is to do more than just create an outline of your speech. You must consider which questions or issues might emerge during your presentation, especially when you are asking questions to invoke audience participation, and be prepared to deal with them. It is fun to be involved in a conversation or giving a presentation when you are well prepared. Then when the responses start coming from the other person or audience, you think to yourself, "*I knew that would probably come up, and I know how to deal with it.*" It actually makes you *smile inside* when you have prepared well in advance.

Should I Use Presentation Aids?

Whether or not you use any presentation aids (*flip charts, white board, Microsoft PowerPoint, graphics, etc.*) is really driven by the circumstances of your presentation. There are basically 3 approaches.

1. Of course, you can use none at all—and this is fine, especially if you are asked to give a presentation on short notice and have no time to prepare any aids, or there is no facility or equipment available.

2. If equipment such as a flip chart or white board are available, and you are presenting to a relatively small group, you can write down key words or short phrases of the points you are making or the ideas you wish to convey to your audience as your presentation evolves.

3. For larger audiences where you have lead time for preparation, you may want to use something like Microsoft PowerPoint with a projection system for your audience to see. The key here is to anticipate how the audience responds to your questions, and then present a short version of the answers or key points after discussion. You can 'build' the slide content during the presentation with animation.

A useful metaphor to apply when listing or presenting the key points of your presentation comes from the popular TV show, **Family Feud**, where the MC says "*In response to the question, 'What are the three most popular ice cream flavors in the USA?' You said, 'Vanilla, Raspberry, and Chocolate.' The audience said, 'Chocolate, Vanilla, and Strawberry'.*" In your presentation you may well get audience feedback that does not correspond exactly with your prepared slides. Then, using the above metaphor you can say "*In our discussion, we came up with these three points* [and list the points]. *We typically get the following responses when asking this question* [and show the list of prepared points]. *As you* *can see, we have a pretty close match."* Then continue with discussion on the mismatches.

The key to successfully using presentation aids in a presentation is to **keep it simple!** Use only key words or very short phrases to sequence or keep track of your content. Avoid using sentences or paragraphs of information with your presentation aids. Use presentation aids primarily to serve as reminders of the presentation content. They can be useful when summarizing at the end or sometimes for back-reference during a Q&A session. The following example is a slide that 'builds' the 4 key reasons for using a *Rephrase* when discussing the *Question/Confusion/ Conflict* Communication Model.

Improving Interpersonal Communication Skills
Questions/Confusion/Conflict Model

Why Rephrase?

1. Validate the communication
2. Create an agreeable mindset
3. Force yourself to listen
4. Allow more time to formulate an answer

When presenting a complex subject with several steps that require a logical progression of thought, presentation aids can be useful to not only help your audience gain understanding, but also to help you keep on track.

What About Personal Aids?

Here's an effective trick to help you prepare and remember the key points of your presentation. Prepare the written outline and key points. Prepare 3 by 5 index cards with the key words to remind you of what you want to discuss. Practice your presentation with your aids. Then, when you actually give your presentation—**don't use them!**

Why? Because you won't need them—they can just get in the way and become a distraction. You have internalized your content during the preparation process.

I have helped many graduate students prepare for presenting their dissertations. They know their material inside and out; however, when they get up to give their presentation, they get a little nervous and start depending heavily on their written notes and subsequently completely lose their audience. On several occasions, I have actually called the presenter over, taken the 3X5 cards or notes, told him or her to just relax and "tell your story, engage your audience"—you've got this material down pat! On every occasion, this resulted in the presenter becoming more relaxed and effective in presenting the material.

Do I Need to Use Body Language?

The body language messages you convey with the non-verbal models still apply—the only difference is that scale becomes more important. You want to predominately convey *Openness*. However, where you might simply show open palms while sitting close to someone in a one-on-one conversation, you need to exaggerate your body language to send a message to a larger audience. If someone is sitting in the back of a large room of several hundred people, you appear much smaller than when up close and personal. By extending your arms while showing open palms and exaggerating your non-verbal messages, you can reach an entire room of people. While exaggerated gesturing may seem unnatural to you at first, it works and adds energy and dynamics to your verbal communication and overall appearance.

Who Do I Look At?

When giving your presentation, it helps if you look slowly left to right and back and forth across the audience. With each view, pick out someone and focus briefly on that person. Magically, the 10-12 people in the audience near that person think you are looking directly at them.

When you are in Q&A mode and responding to a question from the audience, first, repeat the question for the audience (***rephrase*** *and get confirmation from the person asking the question*). Then answer the question while looking directly at the person who asked the question. Sometimes, the answer comes from someone in the audience. In that case, be sure to acknowledge the person who responded, then repeat the answer for the audience while looking at the person who asked the question and ask if the response does, in fact, answer his or her question.

One approach that is frequently mentioned to reduce being nervous when looking at an audience is to "pretend that the audience is naked." I guess the idea is to alleviate your fear of the audience by imagining that 'underneath the pretense of clothing, jewelry, etc., we are all the same'. Another popular *equalizer* is the old saying, 'He puts his pants on one leg at a time, just like I do.' That one works better for me than the former. Let's face it—most people look better with their clothes on.

Basic Speech/Presentation Structure

The primary key to creating an interesting, interactive presentation is to design it to be ***question driven***. Since it can be difficult for many of us to stand and talk continuously for 30 minutes, or more, let the audience become 'the wind beneath your wings'. Ask questions and at the same time gain information that allows you to assess how much your audience already knows. This puts you, as the speaker, on the knowledge level of your audience and you can make adjustments to your content to better fit your audience. If you think about it, the purpose of most speeches or presentations is to share information that answers a compelling question or provides a solution to a problem. Your objective is to do that in the most effective way.

Start With a 'Hook' Question

Depending on the circumstances, you may be introduced by someone else, or you may introduce yourself, if an introduction is needed. In either case, you want to immediately **ask the audience members a compelling question** so they respond or at least think to themselves, **"Yes, I want to know the answer to that question."** That question **hooks** your audience, shifting them into a listening mode.

Then use this question and response to build a **"social contract"** with the audience members that essentially **moves them to want to hear what you have to say**. Let's use our '*John working overtime*' example to illustrate how this set up works. Imagine you are giving a presentation to a group of supervisors or entry level managers about **"How to Communicate More Effectively"** with senior level management regarding work related issues.

> **Your Hook Question:** *"How many of you have had or think you may run into a situation where you need permission from a senior manager to have someone work overtime?"*

After asking the question, you can raise your right arm to indicate a show of hands and you may well get positive verbal responses as well. You've got their attention!

> **Your Social Contract:** *"Would you like to learn effective techniques to help you overcome some challenges you could encounter so you can avoid potential conflict with your boss?"*

Again, you can ask for a show of hands or acknowledge signs of affirmation such as heads nodding or positive verbal responses.

Use the Communication Models in the Body of the Presentation

At this point, you are ready to move into the body of your presentation. And, you can do this by continuing to ask questions. This lets the audience carry the speech for you so you don't have to talk continuously. Again, using our '*John working overtime*' example as an illustration for a presentation on effective communication skills, you could ask:

> **Your Question:** *"What are some of the challenges you might encounter from your manager?"*
> If you don't get any response, you can expand your question by asking the audience to reflect on past experiences and share them.

Answers from the audience could be something like:

> **Audience Response 1:** *"My boss might be concerned that John might not be qualified to do the work by himself during overtime."*
>
> **Audience Response 2:** *"My manager may say that there is not enough money in the budget for overtime."*
>
> **Audience Response 3:** *"The issue with my boss would be the amount of overtime John has been working lately."*

If the audience leaves any challenges out that are important, you can raise those as questions (**direct probes**), for example:

> **Your Question:** *"Might your boss ask that you assign some additional people to the task and get it done today?"*

After you have established the challenges you want to discuss, including some that may have come from the audience that you had not anticipated, you can continue with interactive dialogue, **now focusing on solutions for the challenges**, by asking:

Your Question: *"Assuming John is qualified, how can we overcome the concern that John can't handle working overtime on his own?"*

The possible responses from the audience will range from excellent to poor or even no responses at all. Your job as the speaker is to elicit their input, and work with it using the Communication Models to eventually reveal the information you want to get across. Since this is a dynamic process, you cannot predict the audience response. Fortunately, the models equip you to navigate through their responses and shape them, if necessary, until you are satisfied that your key points have been made.

An excellent response to our question, 'Assuming John is qualified, how can we overcome the concern that John can't handle working overtime on his own?' would be something along these lines:

Audience Response: *"You could reassure your boss by saying, 'Well, we certainly don't want anyone working overtime on a job this important who is not qualified. Please let me assure you that John can handle this work by himself. He has proven himself many times in the past. We can count on John to get the job done'."*

This one is worthy of use in a **Reservation/Doubt Model** as is! All you have to do is to give a positive acknowledgment (**Agreement Model**) to the person's response with, "*Very good!*" Then repeat the response for the entire audience, ask **(Query Model)** for their concurrence and congratulate the audience to build rapport and encourage participation.

Let's say you get a response that approximates what you are looking for such as:

Audience Response: *"You could say John has handled this work in the past."*

In this case the audience is substantiating John's ability but perhaps not in the most diplomatic way. Remember, you are not teaching the communication models per se as your presentation. Nonetheless, you can still apply them and perhaps indirectly educate your audience. For example, you could **reinforce** (**Agreement Model**) the content by saying, "That would establish that John is qualified. Are there any thoughts on how to make it more diplomatic? (**Query Model–indirect probe**)"

Ideally (although not likely unless your audience is familiar with our communication models) you would like a response such as, "*You might say it is important that we have someone qualified before stating John's qualifications* (**reassurance** step of the **Reservation/Doubt Model**). If you should get that response you can **reinforce**.

If there is no response you could simply ask (**Query Model-direct probe**) your audience, "*Before stating John's qualifications, do you think it would be a good idea to let your boss know you share his or her concern by saying something like: 'Well it is certainly important that we have someone qualified to handle the task. The reason John was suggested is ...'.*"

What if you get a poor or incomplete response, such as:

> **Audience Response:** "*You could say no one else is available.*"

What communication model fits this response? **Question/ Confusion/Conflict?** Right! You could respond with, "*So you're saying there is no other option?*" You can then use the **Query model** starting with **indirect probes** to see if this is a good idea by asking something such as, "*Do you think this will be satisfactory to management?*" You'll probably get "*not likely*" as an answer; then you can ask for other thoughts and hope the *collective wisdom* of the audience can come up with a better response. If the audience is still struggling switch to **direct probes** and say something like, "*Would it help to point out John's experience or training?* Or, "*What if I can be available by telephone if John has a problem?*"

What if your audience does not respond at all? What do you do? If you replied, use the **Query Model** with **direct probing** you are correct. You could say, "*Would it help to let your boss know you* *share his or her concern by saying something like, 'Well it is certainly important that we have someone qualified,' to demonstrate you understand your boss's concern; then review John's experience and/or qualifications?"*

As your audience picks up on the idea and correctly adds to it, you can **reinforce** and **expand** with the **Agreement Model**.

By using questions you can encourage the audience to work with you to come up with answers.

> **Your Question:** *"How can we overcome the fact that there is not enough money left in the budget for John to work overtime?"*

Someone in the audience may well respond with:

> **Audience Response:** *"You could always ask the boss, 'Would it be better to take a hit for exceeding our overtime budget, or get in trouble for being late delivering paychecks to our 5,000 employees?'"*

Again, you can give positive acknowledgement for the response, then repeat it for the entire audience, pointing out how presenting the lesser of two evils (so to speak) puts things in perspective for the boss (**Question/Confusion/Conflict Model–minimization**) was used to put the situation in perspective when dealing with **conflict**. Since the audience response did not include a **rephrase** of the manager's objection, you could ask the audience: *"Do you think it would be useful to rephrase the boss' objection before responding to make sure you clearly understood what he said?"*

Do you see how we use the **Explanation Model [problem/ solution]** along with the **Query Model [indirect and direct probes]** for the structure of the presentation? Your questions are designed to elicit both the problems and solutions from the audience while you facilitate and add additional content and relevant comments.

Then you are ready to continue with the body of your presentation using questions and answers, following the problem/ solution format to generate discussion about all of the challenges raised.

Ending a Speech

How do you end a speech or presentation? Let the audience do the close for you. You can do this by asking the audience questions that recall the key points or challenges presented in the speech and how to address those challenges. You can do this with or without a visual aid such as Microsoft PowerPoint. When using PowerPoint, simply withhold presenting the answers to your questions until the audience has answered most if not all of the summary questions.

If you present with visual aids, be certain to mention any audience contributions that occurred during the presentation and add salient remarks to tie everything together. Finally, you should discuss any action items that may have emerged during the presentation (**Close Model**).

Do you see how this works? This interactive approach allows you to:

1. Tap into the *collective wisdom* of the audience, which may provide responses for 50% or more of the issues discussed in the presentation.

2. Learn new ideas to incorporate into future presentations from the audience points that you had not considered.

3. Be more relaxed as you give your presentation because you don't feel like you have to know everything. You can just ask your audience!

4. Become more of a facilitator or teaching guru rather than a stoic, unilateral, boring formal speaker.

Following is a template to help you gain an overall perspective on creating a presentation based on the approach in this Chapter.

TEMPLATE USING COMMUNICATION MODELS FOR PRESENTATIONS

Speaker Introduction: May or may not occur depending on whether or not necessary.

Hook Question: Must be designed to pique the interest of most if not all of your audience.

Social Contract: Sets up your commitment to the audience to answer the hook question.

Body of Presentation: There are a couple of approaches that you can use to develop discussion around the challenges generated with the *hook question* and fulfilling your *social contract*.

1. Use questions to generate discussion to create a list of challenges identified by the hook question; then go back and ask questions to identify or formulate solutions for each of the challenges.

2. Or, you can use questions to generate discussion to reveal a specific challenge, then continue with questions to have the audience (with your prompting if necessary) come up with one or more viable solutions. Finally move on to the next challenge/solution discussion.

The basic framework for building the body of the presentation looks like:

> **Issue / Problem #1:**
> **Solution #1:**
>
> **Issue / Problem #2:**
> **Solution #2:**
> -
> -
> -

Use appropriate communication models to manage the flow of the discussion and to make key points. If you receive:

- ➢ Agreement, then reinforce and expand.
- ➢ Reservation or Doubt, then Reassure and Substantiate.
- ➢ Conflict, then Rephrase and Minimize (or compromise if necessary).
- ➢ Confusion, then Rephrase and Clarify.
- ➢ Question, then Rephrase and Answer.

Close: Review Problems & Solutions
            Propose Course of Action(s), if any

Thank the Audience for their attention and participation.

Flesh out this basic template with your relevant comments and observations along with pertinent discussion to make your presentation flow. For example, during your presentation be sure to use the **Agreement Model (Reinforce & Expand)** when someone says something supportive. Should an audience member ask a **question**, be sure to **rephrase** (and get affirmation on your rephrase) so all can hear the question, then **answer** the question while making eye contact with the person who asked.

Applying the Presentation Template

As you can see, the verbal and non-verbal communication models presented in this book, become very useful tools for preparing and effectively delivering a speech or presentation. The following is a speech prepared using the above template. The key components of the presentation are on the left side in bold and pertinent comments are italicized in brackets [ ] so you can see how the models are applied. The "Answers" provided in the dialogue are what you might expect to receive based on my experience in giving this presentation many times previously. You can always ask questions to lead the audience to approximate the correct answers.

Note: The following speech is a composite of information derived from several articles on the Internet.

Speech Example

USEFUL TIPS FOR AVOIDING SPEEDING TICKETS

Introduction: Good morning! I appreciate the opportunity to be with you today. My name is [*your name here*] and I'm here to share some information you may find very useful sometime in the future.

Hook Question: How many of you know someone who has received a speeding ticket or have you personally been pulled over and given a ticket for speeding? [*When asking this question, raise your right hand as an indication of what people in the audience should do in response.*]

Comment: Not a pleasant experience is it?

Social Contract: Would you like some useful guidelines and tips on what you can do to either avoid or reduce your chances of getting a speeding ticket should you find yourself being stopped by a police officer for speeding?
[*Again, raise your right hand as an indication of what the audience should do in response.*]

Comment: Let's say you are going 80 mph in a 65 mph speed zone and you are picked up on the radar of an officer coming from the opposite direction—and he decides to pursue you. Please note that I refer to the law enforcement officer as male, but the same applies for female officers as well.

Question: Now, does it make sense to put yourself in the position of the officer to gain some perspective on the situation?

Question: What is the oncoming officer going to have to do if he decides to pursue you?

Answer: First, he has to make a U-turn and speed up to over 90 mph, maybe weaving in and out of traffic, to catch you, even if you have slowed down to 65 mph.

Question: Do you think this might have some impact on the amount of adrenalin pumping through his body? [*You will get a positive response from the audience.*]

Question: Another useful consideration is the officer's motivation. What do you think are the two primary driving forces behind his behavior at this time? Let me give you some hints ...

Question: Why do you think most police officers chose to be in law enforcement? [*You may get several responses from the audience; you want to focus on the following, even if you have to provide it.*]

Answer: Most people get into law enforcement because they want to be "the man"—the person who is in charge and telling others what to do.

Question: What do you think the officer might be thinking when walking up to the side of your car once you have pulled over to the side of the road? From another perspective, what do you think is of most concern of an officer's spouse when he or she leaves for work every day? [*Again, you may get several responses from the audience; you want to focus on the following, even if you have to provide it.*]

Answer: When approaching your car, the officer might be concerned about being hit by traffic speeding by as he is doing his job. He might also fear that this could be the time someone would pull out a gun and start shooting at him.

Comment: You've got it! On one hand the officer wants to be respected, representing the law, and on the other hand he is fearful that the situation could be dangerous or violent. [*At this point, you have established a problem.*]

Question: After pulling over, what do you think most people do while the officer is walking up to the side of the car?

Answer: Probably fumbling around in his or her pocket or purse trying to find their drivers license or reaching over and searching through their glove box for your proof of insurance and vehicle registration.

Question: Could this behavior be a cause for concern for the officer?

Answer: Absolutely, for all he knows, the driver is reaching for some kind of weapon.

Question: Given this, what are some things you can do to reduce the officer's level of fear and show respect? [*Now, we are looking for solution(s) for the above problem.*]

Answer: Pull way off the road to give him room for safety when approaching your car.

Answer: Roll your window down, especially if it is heavily tinted. If it is at night, also immediately turn on your interior light. Show you have nothing to hide.

Answer: Extend your arms out over your steering wheel with palms open. This is a sign of submissiveness—hands up. Do not do anything that may be perceived as a threat!

[Give a positive acknowledgement to the people in the audience as they contribute their answers and be sure to repeat them so the entire audience hears what was said.]

[At this point, we have several actions that provide a solution for the threat problem.]

Question: Does it matter to an officer what branch of law enforcement he is in along with his rank?

Answer: Indeed it does.

Question: Could you show the officer respect by addressing him by his title and/or rank?

Question: How can we tell what branch of service an officer might be in and what his rank is?

Corporal? One or two stripes.
Sergeant? Three or more stripes.
Trooper? No stripes and in a State Police car.
Deputy? No stripes in a County car.

If you are not sure, go with Officer! I recommend you check out your local law enforcement uniforms for rank indicators.

Question: Do you think it is a good idea to politely greet the officer with something like "Good afternoon Officer" and let him take it from there or to just keep quiet if you are pulled over for a traffic violation?

[You can get some mixed responses for this question, depending on peoples' experience.]

Question: How might being silent be interpreted?

Answer: It could be taken as an admission of guilt.

Comment: Exactly! This is the time to be polite and courteous. Avoid being rude, self-righteous or indignant with the officer. That does more harm than good.

Question: Given any dialogue, is the officer impressed by honesty or by attempts at deception?

Answer: Honesty.

Question: What is a key point to remember if you feel the need to stretch the truth a little bit to convince the officer to let you go with just a warning?

Answer: Keep your explanation plausible. If the officer thinks you trying to *pull a fast one*, you are just wasting your time.

Question: Do you think that an experienced officer has heard just about every excuse in the book before?

Answer: Most likely.

Question: Would you like to hear one of the most unusual excuses I have heard for trying to get out of a ticket? *[Anticipate a positive response and continue with:]* This guy was stopped for excessive speeding and questioned by the officer as to why he was going so fast. He replied, "I was divorced six months ago and heard that my ex-wife married a cop. I thought it might be you and you were

trying to chase me down and give her back to me!"
Humorous maybe, but it didn't work.

Question: Given that an officer's primary motivators are to be
respected and to feel safe, do you think the
behaviors mentioned above could have some
influence on whether or not the officer decides to
give you a ticket or let you go with a warning?

Answer: You bet!

*[The above discussion is more about avoiding a
potential problem caused by poor interpersonal
interaction rather than being faced with having a
problem. Let's call it a problem avoidance
solution.]*

Question: Do any of you in the audience have any interesting
stories about speeding tickets that you would like
to share?

*[There are usually one or two people from the
audience who have an interesting contribution to
share with the audience. The stories sometimes
reinforce your comments or provide back-reference
material for later on in your presentation or in
future presentations.]*

Comment: Here's one for you: A guy driving with his wife in
the front passenger seat gets pulled over. The
man realizes that he does not have his seat belt
on, so he quickly straps it on before the police
officer walks up to his car.

The officer says, "Sir, do you know why I pulled
you over?"

The man says, "No sir, I am sure I was driving under the speed limit."

The officer says, "You're right, you were not speeding; however, when I passed you coming from the opposite direction, I noticed that you were not wearing your seat belt. That is why I pulled you over."

"But officer, I am wearing my seat belt!" exclaims the man.

"Yes sir, you are now. But you were not wearing it when I passed you a few minutes ago." says the officer.

The man protests again saying, "You must be mistaken, I was wearing my seat belt."

The officer says to the man's wife, "Excuse me ma'am, do you have anything to say about this situation?"

The man's wife says, "Yes sir, I've learned that it is no use trying to argue with my husband when he's been drinking!"

[*The above story always generates a good round of laughter after which you can continue with the following comment.*]

Coaching Tip:

Using humor in a presentation can be effective in engaging the audience and keeping them interested in what you are saying, as long as the humor is relevant. Telling a joke, even though it may be very funny, is a distraction rather than a complement to a presentation if it is not relevant.

The best use of humor is to tell a funny story or anecdote that illustrates a point you are making in the speech.

Comment: A well trained officer has made a decision about giving you a ticket before he gets out of his patrol car. However, to make their jobs a bit more interesting, many officers wait to hear your side of the story or take time to evaluate the circumstances before making a final decision about whether or not to give you a ticket.

Question: What can you do to decrease your chances of getting a ticket?

[*You may be able to refer back to some audience stories at this point. If not, continue with the following question if it has not already been mentioned.*]

Question: I don't mean to be sexist here, but if you are a female, does it help to cry? [*The audience generally responds with "Yes."*]

Comment: In many cases it does! If the officer is a man, a woman crying may make him feel sorry for her and let her go with just a warning.

Comment: Based on the research I've done, it appears that women get excused from getting tickets more than men do. You may have heard about the instructor for a remedial driving course that walks into the class and says, "Hey, where are all the ladies?" [*This last sentence needs to be made with a smile and a sense of humor as you are trying to tell a subtle joke.*]

Question: What do you think? [*This question can sometimes create some lively discussion/debate in the audience.*]

Question: Here's an interesting point of information for you. Do you know why women appear to cry easier than men? [*Again, this question usually generates some lively discussion.*]

Answer: Well, based on a research study discussed by Diane Sawyer on the ABC **Good Morning America** show, women appear to cry easier than men do because their tears are physically channeled to run down their cheeks while the tear ducts in males just cause the eyes to water. The study also points out that after the age of 11 years, the ratio of crying episodes is 5 times more for females than men.

Question: Would you like to know a technique that may well convince the oncoming officer not to turn around and chase you down in the first place? [*This is where you answer the 'hook' question.*]

Question: Well, what is your 'knee jerk' reaction as the officer passes you coming from the opposite direction? [*You may get several responses to this question, but be sure and include the following answer.*]

Answer: You put on the brakes causing your tail lights to light up, indicating that you indeed must have been speeding. And, you look straight ahead, avoiding eye contact, hoping that the officer just didn't notice that you were going too fast.

Comment: Of course, that behavior just makes you look even more guilty! [*This could also be asked as a question.*]

Comment: What you should do is look directly at the officer as he is approaching/passing you and give him a salute or a wave of acknowledgement! [This comment usually generates some puzzling looks.]

Question: Why do you think this might keep him from turning around and pursuing you?

[*Most audiences cannot answer this correctly at first—go ahead and acknowledge efforts to answer the question. If no one responds correctly, continue probing the audience, holding off awhile before giving the answer to build SUSPENSE!*]

Comment: Here's the answer: The reason he may not pursue you is because only another officer would do this! The salute or gentle wave and a nod is what an off-duty officer would do to acknowledge another officer that he just realized he was speeding and immediately slowed down.

That behavior sends the message that, 'Hey, I'm in law enforcement too. I know I'm speeding and I'll slow it down.' As a professional courtesy, officers generally don't give each other tickets.

[*As in 'normal' conversation, there is value in asking a question the audience cannot answer. Then, when the answer is revealed, the listener gains appreciation and becomes convinced that the conversation, or in this case, speech was worthwhile.*]

[*At this point, you have essentially fulfilled your social contract with your audience and are ready to end the speech using the **Close Model**.*]

[*This Socratic or dialectic method of learning using questions and answers to lead to a rational response is a powerful way to reinforce the recall of the audience when they are trying to remember the key points of the speech at a later time.*]

Comment: I certainly hope this information proves useful to you should you find yourself being pulled over for speeding. Of course, I have to say that the surest way to avoid a speeding ticket is to stay at or below the posted speed limit.

But you and I both know that sometimes that can be dangerous when the surrounding traffic is *flying* by you 10 to 15 mph above the speed limit. A relatively safe approach is to not exceed the speed limit by more than 5 mph. Using the cruise control that is on most cars these days can help you stay within the 5 mph limit. (I am talking about interstate highways here, not school zones!)

I often get asked, "What should I say if I try the salute techniques, and get pulled over anyway, and he asks me why I gave him a salute?" Simply say that you were acknowledging the fact that you had been caught and were looking for a place to safely pull over. Tell him it was a sign of respect, as it should be. Never claim to be in law enforcement unless you really are.

Comment: As a quick review before closing, what are some of the key points we discussed during this presentation? [*At this point, you want the audience to summarize the key points, with your guidance if necessary.*]

Answer:　If the officer is coming from the opposite direction, slow down without braking, look at the officer and give a salute or wave of acknowledgement. He may consider you a fellow officer and not pursue you.

Answer:　If you are pursued, consider the mindset of the officer at the time (wants to be the one in control and may well be somewhat fearful—depending upon your actions).

Answer:　Pull well off the road to allow the officer to safely approach your car.

Answer:　Put both hands with open palms in view on the top of your steering wheel.

Answer:　Be polite and greet the officer by rank and branch of service if you can identify it—don't try to fabricate some story that is obviously not true. The best policy is to be honest and if you think it could be helpful, briefly explain why you were exceeding the speed limit.

[Give a positive acknowledgement to the people in the audience as they contribute their answers and be sure to repeat them so the entire audience hears what was said. Make sure that all of the key points are reviewed even if you have to bring them up yourself.]

Comment:　One last thing, never underestimate the power of a question. As a last resort, you can always say; "Officer, I am terribly sorry I was driving over the speed limit. I really cannot afford to get a ticket much less the impact it will have on the cost of my insurance. Would it be possible for you to give me a warning citation rather than giving me a ticket?"

It may not get you out of a ticket, but he may at least charge you with a lesser offense than what he originally planned.

Comment: Thank you for your attention and participation. I hope these tips and techniques prove useful should you ever need them.

[End of speech]

Do you see how the communication models apply to giving a speech or presentation? Using questions reduces your stress level and increases audience attention and participation. The process of giving a presentation becomes much more relaxed and enjoyable.

Scoring Points Through Presentations

The title of this chapter included the notion of scoring points through presentations. What is that all about? I can't emphasize enough the importance and value of being able to comfortably give a speech or presentation. As discussed early in this Chapter, most people are intimidated or fearful of having to get up in front of an audience and speak. By learning and practicing the communication models presented in this book and applying them to the presentation process, you overcome your fears and actually enjoy giving speeches and presentations as well as facilitating important business meetings or social gatherings.

What should you do when an opportunity presents itself to give a presentation? While everyone else is nervously avoiding eye contact and hoping to "dodge the bullet," seize the day! Step up and volunteer to give the presentation or facilitate a meeting. You now have the tools to prepare for such occasions. If you are ready, willing and able to step up to the plate when everyone else is fearful, does that signal to others that you are a leader? You become the 'chosen one' to speak and represent all the others.

Having had the privilege to serve on the Board of Directors for several companies, including Best Buy and Ciber, I can assure you that the people most considered and chosen for promotion and leadership positions are the ones who excel at presenting information in a clear, logical, and comfortable manner. Boards of directors often first become aware of a rising talent in the company when they make a presentation to the Board. A great presentation is often followed by questions from Board members such as, "How long has that person been with us? What are her current responsibilities? Is she being groomed for higher leadership roles? Or even better, is she in the CEO candidate pool?

Would you like to have questions such as these asked about you?

Write to express rather than impress.
Use short sentences and paragraphs along with familiar words
in an active voice.

17

Making Your Point Through Persuasive Written Communication

"Can I use these communication models to improve my effectiveness when communicating in writing through email messages, memos, letters and reports?" is a question frequently asked by our seminar participants. As with our response to using the models for speeches and presentations, the answer is a definite **yes**.

However, when writing, the useful non-verbal tools and cues of body language, facial expressions, tone and interaction are not in play. The writer must use extra care to ensure clarity and avoid misunderstandings. Important tip—because you lose the impact of non-verbal tools, a friendly message can come across as harsh. For example, a simple email such as "I need to review your status report" can sound demanding or even angry. Simply changing that to, "Would you please provide your status report for review?" shifts the dynamics to a pleasant request.

Strategy for Success

An unfortunate and typical mistake made in written communication is lack of preparation. Too often in the rush of the day, we write something down and send it off without considering how our message might be received or misunderstood.

In the same way you prepare for a critical interpersonal encounter, a group presentation or a speech, you prepare written communication by sharing ideas with colleagues and even the recipient(s) to discover whether they have questions, reservations or doubts, confusion or even areas of potential conflict. This enables interactively discussing, considering, negotiating, agreeing upon or understanding issues in advance. It is always easier to "take something back" during a discussion than to try to withdraw information already in print.

As you fine tune your message, you can have others review it to ensure you are communicating the correct message clearly, persuasively and diplomatically. Frequently, the purpose for *written* communication is to document *verbal* communication "for the record" or future reference.

"What if you are not able to interact with the intended recipient of your message?" you ask. Just as when preparing for an important meeting, ask trusted friends and colleagues to give you the feedback you need to make sure you have considered all the issues that your document might elicit from the intended audience.

You will be amazed at how helpful a second pair of eyes is when writing. When I work at home responding to important emails, I ask my wife to read my emails before I send them. I am surprised by and grateful for how she frequently suggests a simple change that makes the message clearer.

Basic Format for Communicating in Writing

The *Explanation Model* (Problem/Solution) is a powerful tool to communicate with the reader in writing. It informs the reader you intend to provide a solution to the problem or question, if the problem is presented as a question.

Have you ever been confused or frustrated while reading because you could not figure out what the author was trying to say? If you recall from the guidelines for using the Explanation Model in Chapter 5, it is important to:

> ➢ Complete the explanation of the problem before you discuss the solution
> ➢ Make sure there is a logical progression of thought to the explanation
> ➢ Lead to an impact statement to complete the problem before presenting the solution(s)

You want your explanation of the problem and the solution to be clear, concise and as straightforward or simple as possible to avoid frustration and confusion for the reader.

After your explanation model, you can address the anticipated concerns (i.e., potential questions, reservations or conflict) of your reader through use of rhetorical questions. Your answers to the anticipated concerns different readers might have provide the dynamics of group interaction. That is, the rhetorical questions serve the same purpose as engaging the audience when giving a presentation. As the reader reviews the rhetorical questions, he or she can decide if an issue is of concern and if the response you provided is acceptable. If the response is acceptable, you satisfied the reader; if not, more communication, oral or written, may be necessary.

This approach is similar to providing FAQs (Frequently Asked Questions) in a technical document or on a web site. The reader has the advantage of learning the answers to his or her concerns as well as those that might have been raised by others.

Responding to Rhetorical Questions with the Communication Models

As you move into the body of your document and express concerns through the use of rhetorical questions, you may respond using the protocol of the appropriate communication model. However, there are **two variations** that occur: reassurance with the *reservation/doubt* model and rephrasing with the *question/confusion/conflict* model are not necessary as the related rhetorical question serves that purpose.

For example, a **reservation/doubt** rhetorical question is, "Do you think John has the necessary experience to handle this task over the weekend?" A response such as, "John has handled this task by himself on six previous occasions. He has the experience and is very responsible" is an example of **reassurance**.

A rhetorical question such as: "How do we cover the cost when we don't have a budget for overtime?" should be treated as **question/confusion/conflict**. A response such as, "The Accounting Department said it is their mistake and they will cover the cost" is an **answer** to that question. A response such as, "Though we don't have money earmarked in the budget, we are allowed to substitute travel funds" is **clarification** for confusion. A response such as, "Though we don't have overtime budget, is it better to have a budget exception or have employees not get paid?" is an example of **minimization** for a conflict.

You may find it helpful to review Chapter 8 for how to handle **reservation/doubt** and Chapter 9 on how to handle **question/ confusion conflict**.

As in conversational use of the communication models, sometimes an issue raised may actually be positive, in which case the **Agreement Model** is applicable. For example, let's say the issue is, "Since the Accounting Department caused the problem shouldn't they cover the cost?" If the Accounting Department has agreed to cover the cost, your written response is, "Yes, and they have agreed to do so," using the **Agreement Model**.

Use the Closure Model to Wrap Things Up

After you have presented the explanation model(s) and provided responses to anticipated concerns, you are ready to summarize and close your document. By using the **Closure Model**, you simply review the key points or objectives of your communication and the course of action or outcome you wish to achieve.

Make It Interesting

Keeping a reader's interest is challenging. Would you like some techniques that can make your written communication more engaging?

The first technique is to use short paragraphs, even single sentence paragraphs, to emphasize a point. Shorter sentences along with familiar words are key parts of this kind of communication. Write to **express**, rather than to **impress**.

The second technique is to use an **active** voice rather than a **passive** voice. Most people tend to use a passive voice in written communication. Using an active voice brings the subject into the action. The following examples point out the difference between the two:

➢ Example 1:

- Passive Voice: By using an active voice, the subject is brought into action.
- Active Voice: Using an active voice brings the subject into the action.

➢ Example 2:

- Passive Voice: You have been asked to write a report.
- Active Voice: Management asked you to write a report.

➢ Example 3:

- Passive Voice: Low morale has resulted in a significant impact on productivity.
- Active Voice: Productivity is at an all time low due to low morale.

After preparing your initial draft of a document, especially one that could have important consequences, ask several friends or close colleagues to read it to confirm that you:

> ➤ Created a logical progression of thought
> ➤ Used clear and concise wording
> ➤ Included and addressed potential concerns using rhetorical questions
> ➤ Crafted short sentences, paragraphs and familiar wording
> ➤ Used an active voice rather than a passive voice
> ➤ Sufficiently reviewed the key points and expected outcome of your communication

As with Chapter 16, **Making Your Point & Scoring Points Through Presentation Skills**, we are including a template to help you gain an overall perspective on creating a written document based on the approach discussed in this Chapter.

TEMPLATE FOR USING COMMUNICATION MODELS FOR WRITING

Author Introduction: May or may not be needed depending on the formality of the document.

State the Subject of the Document: Can be in the form of a compelling *question* for which you are providing an *answer*, or a *problem* for which you are providing a *solution* (the Explanation Model).

Body of Document: The primary approach for developing the body of your document is to point out **reservation/doubts** and **question/ confusion/conflict** in the form of rhetorical questions.

Provide the appropriate response to each question.

By using rhetorical questions, you stimulate reader interest in the challenges raised by the hook question. You do the same when addressing each challenge with a rhetorical question, then following up each challenge by providing solutions.

Closure: Review Problems & Solutions
Propose Course of Action(s) as appropriate

Using this basic template, you can build an initial outline of your document, and set up the key points you want to make and develop with a logical progression of thought for your narrative.

Putting It to Work
Example One: Business Correspondence

Now that we have covered some fundamentals for adapting the verbal communication models to written communication, let's use the need to have John work overtime again—only this time you are requesting permission from your manager in writing via an email message.

As you prepare to write the email to your manager/boss to have John work overtime, think of some of the challenges you might encounter from your boss. For example, your boss might say:

1. "There is not enough money in the overtime budget to pay for overtime."
2. "No way, John has been working too much overtime lately."
3. "Can't we just put more people on the task and get it done today?"

Those are certainly valid objections or concerns that your boss could have, so let's address them in your initial request before they become an issue.

As you read through the following example of a *written conversation*, see if you can identify the various verbal communication models used in the written conversation.

Date: Friday 1:30 P.M.

From: You

To: Manager

Subject: Request for Overtime

Have you heard about the situation with payroll?

If not, here is a quick update.

The payroll transactions came in late from the Accounting Department today and there is not enough time to get them processed so people can get paid on Monday. John is available and willing to work overtime this weekend to solve the problem.

Is it OK with you to schedule him for overtime Saturday morning?

To assist in making your decision, here are a few issues for your review and consideration.

First, can we put more people on the task and get it done today and avoid overtime?

We would certainly exercise that option if that were possible. However, this is a linear task that requires several sequential steps that unfortunately cannot be done in parallel. Also, there is simply not enough time left today to get the job done. Does this help clarify the situation?

Second, is there enough money in the overtime budget to cover this expense?

Unfortunately, our overtime budget is depleted. However, I checked with the Accounting Department and we can transfer enough funds from our travel budget to cover the overtime expense. While this has an impact on our future travel capabilities, do you think it is better than missing a critical deadline when you consider senior management's perspective?

Third, how much overtime has John put in lately?

I know you are concerned about employee "burn out" due to how much overtime we ask them to work. Prior to checking with John to see if he was available, I checked his overtime record and it has been over two months since he has worked overtime. John is eager for the overtime opportunity.

Since the transactions are late, we want to get people paid on time, John is available and we have a way to cover the cost, is it OK to proceed?

What if your boss responds with the following message . . .

Date: Friday 2:00 P.M.

From: Manager

To: You

Subject: Request for Overtime

It looks like you have done a thorough job of assessing our situation. My only concern is whether or not John has the qualifications to handle processing the payroll transactions on his own over the weekend.

I really get sick and tired of cleaning up after the Accounting Department's mistakes. I wish there were something we could do about that. Do you have any ideas?

Then you can respond with . . .

Date: Friday 2:10 P.M.

From: You

To: Manager

Subject: Request for Overtime

Thank you for your prompt response and expressing your concerns about qualifications.

We certainly don't want anyone processing the payroll transactions that is not qualified. John has handled payroll processing on his own several times in the past and is well qualified to do the job on his own. We can count on John. Additionally, I will be available just in case something unexpected comes up while he is working. Does that make you more comfortable?

Regarding the Accounting Department mistake, I spoke with the Department Director, explained the situation and the impact it had on us, and received an apology along with approval to bill their Department for the overtime costs. The Accounting Department will be sending a follow up email to our conversation on Monday. Does that work for you?

Given John's experience, my availability to back him up and Accounting's willingness to "pay for their mistake," may we proceed with John working overtime?

Your boss responds with . . .

Date: Friday 2:20 P.M.

From: Manager

To: You

Subject: Request for Overtime

Thanks for sharing your confidence in John and being on standby in case something comes up. I appreciate you taking the initiative in working with the Accounting Department to cover the overtime expense. If you think about it, that is only fair since the problem is their fault.

You have my approval to go ahead with scheduling John for overtime.

Again, thanks for all you do!

Do you see how the verbal communication models are applied in the example above? By using the communication models in your writing, you can communicate more clearly and diplomatically in a manner that avoids misunderstandings.

Putting It to Work
Example Two: Management Report

In most cases when using email or memos for written correspondence, the format is more conversational and informal. A written report, such as a Management Report, generally has more content and is more formally structured. Reports are typically ten to twenty pages but can be hundreds of pages long. In many cases, the intended readers for these reports are very busy people and quite frankly, do not take the time to read the report, but rather skim over it quickly looking for the *high points*.

To make sure that the salient points of a report catch the reader's attention requires an expanded template or format. The most significant differences between informal written correspondence and a formal written report are leading with an *Executive Summary* followed by a *Table of Contents*.

The Executive Summary succinctly addresses the critical content such as the problem and alternatives and includes the recommendations developed in the report. If the recommendations are acceptable to management, they often don't read or study the report.   If the recommendations are questionable, the report provides the details to back up the recommendations. The table of contents directs the reader to specific sections that may be of importance to understanding the recommendations.

The executive summary is similar to someone telling you how a book ends before you read it! That would usually be objectionable but to management it can be a great time saver.

Though perhaps obvious, you generally complete the *Executive Summary* and *Table of Contents* last when preparing a report. Why? Because until the analysis and report are complete the recommendations are hard to summarize. The same can happen with section headings and page numbers.

The *Executive Summary* appears at the beginning of the report and succinctly addresses the critical content such as a description of the problem along with the recommended solution. Giving the reader the *essence* of the report, the *Executive Summary* is quick and easy to read. Then, if the reader wants additional information, he or she can either read the full report, or access a specific section based on the *Table of Contents*. The following outline provides a useful structure or template for a formal report.

> ➢ Report Title Page
> ➢ Executive Summary
> ➢ Table of Contents
> ➢ Introduction
> ➢ Background Information
> ➢ Alternatives Considered
> ➢ Findings
> ➢ Recommendations and Justifications
> ➢ Summary

Preparing a formal Management Report using the verbal communication models and the structure discussed above is our second example.

Here is the situation:

Your organization is experiencing an increase in turnover rate. Over the past couple of years, more and more people have left your Company and either gone to work for your competition or into completely different occupations. Overall morale is down and so is productivity.

The Company CEO and the Senior Management Team asked you to lead a Performance Management Task Team to research the Company's serious employee retention and low morale problems and recommend a solution to improve overall morale and productivity. They have asked you to provide them with a written report that includes your findings and recommendations along with supporting justification. The following report is an example of how you might write your report.

**IMPROVING EMPLOYEE MORALE
AND PRODUCTIVITY
Research, Findings and Recommendations**

Prepared by

The Performance Management Task Team

for

**The Chief Executive Officer
and
The Senior Management Team**

<u>*Page 1: Management Report Example*</u>

IMPROVING EMPLOYEE MORALE
AND PRODUCTIVITY

Research, Findings and Recommendations

Prepared by the Performance Management Task Team

Table of Contents

<u>*Page 2: Management Report Example*</u>

IMPROVING EMPLOYEE MORALE AND PRODUCTIVITY

Research, Findings and Recommendations

Executive Summary

This report, prepared for the senior management team at the direction of our CEO, addresses the significant employee retention issues we have experienced over the past several years along with the measurable decrease in overall morale, productivity and profitability.

The research and investigation, upon which this report is based, revealed that the root cause of our retention and morale problems is an ineffective incentive and reward program. Specifically, the varied and ever-changing motivational needs of our employees are not being met with our current program, primarily because those needs are different for each individual and they have not been consistently and accurately identified.

To be able to identify the motivational needs of our employees and gain deeper insight and understanding of how to meet those needs, we strongly recommend **Motivator**®, an interactive tool available through the Internet. The Motivator tool:

- Identifies individual motivational needs;

- Facilitates effective communication between managers and employees about those needs;

- Provides a framework for aligning meaningful incentives and rewards with our organizational goals and objectives; and,

- Is a cost effective solution.

<u>*Page 3: Management Report Example*</u>

IMPROVING EMPLOYEE MORALE AND PRODUCTIVITY
Research, Findings and Recommendations

Introduction

During the past several years, our employee turnover rate increased from an annual industry norm of 5% to an alarming 15%. In addition, our most recent Organizational Climate Survey completed six weeks ago, indicates that overall employee morale is at an all time low. Consequently, productivity has suffered dramatically and is an imminent threat to our Company's stock value and stock holder confidence.

Our Chief Executive Officer requested that we assemble a Performance Management Task Team comprised of middle-level managers from each of our six departments to research, investigate and identify the root cause of the decline in the morale of our employees and their productivity.

Background Information

After forming the task team, we conducted several focus groups with employees throughout our organization and interviewed previous employees who were high-performers that left the Company during the past two years. In these meetings and interviews, we opened with discussion on the overall goals and objectives of our Company, then narrowed the discussion so our employees and interview participants really focused on what was needed to reduce turnover and improve morale and productivity.

After reviewing the detailed notes and recordings of these focus group session and interviews, we were able to isolate the following four key components that our current and past

Page 4: Management Report Example

employees believe are necessary for high morale and productivity:

1. Aptitude
2. Training
3. Technology
4. Motivation

Alternatives Considered

Armed with the knowledge gained through analysis of the focus groups and interview sessions, we considered each of the four key productivity components and how they are currently being managed and administered on our Company.

1. *Aptitude* (Are we placing employees in jobs they are capable of performing?)

With the help of our Human Resources Department we reviewed our recruiting program, initial screening process, aptitude assessment, interview scheduling, and employee negotiation process. Each of the steps is well organized and is integrated with the needs of our senior and middle level managers.

2. *Training* (Are we providing the education and knowledge for employees to do their jobs?)

Our Training Department shared our overall Company education programs for employee training, career development and succession planning. All employees have an Individual Development Plan that is consistent with their current position requirements and their career development ambitions.

3. *Technology* (Are we providing the technology and tools for employees to effectively and efficiently perform their jobs?)

Page 5: Management Report Example

The Information Systems and Technology Support Department gave us a detailed briefing on how they work with the Training Department and Department Managers to make sure that our technology needs are well understood and that our employees have state-of-the-art ergonomic technology along the with proper training to be as productive at possible.

4. **Motivation** (Are we fulfilling the motivational needs of our employees on an individual or personal basis?)

We conducted a focus group with members of the Human Resources Department and several senior and middle managers from each Department in our Company to discuss our current employee incentive and reward program. *Pay for performance* is the primary basis of our current program. Employees who are high achievers or who have demonstrated outstanding performance receive salary step-increases within a position description or periodic bonuses.

Findings

After conducting six focus groups with 55 current employees and interviews with 20 previous employees, we identified four key components that must be in place and successfully aligned with the goals and objectives of our Company for high employee morale and productivity to exist. Our meeting with key leaders and managers throughout our Company to corroborate our interview results and review current practices, policies and procedures, indicates that we are indeed:

1. doing an excellent job in fitting the right people in the right job;
2. teaching the requisite skills and knowledge for our employees to succeed; and,
3. providing the tools and technologies to do the job effectively and efficiently.

Page 6: Management Report Example

Where we are falling woefully short is in the 4th essential component, *Motivation*: fulfilling the motivational needs of our employees on an individual or personal basis. Our current incentive and reward program focuses primarily on employee compensation and does not accommodate other needs such as recognition, achievement, work relationships, leisure or flex-time needs, and other motivational needs.

This is a common problem in many companies. Managers, lacking any other solid information, seem to think that their employees either have the same motivational needs that the managers do or assume the safest strategy is to simply offer more compensation; and they mistakenly bias their rewards to employees. When motivating our employees, it turns out that "Do unto others as you would have them do unto you" is not usually applicable. Instead, "Do unto others as they want done unto them at this point in their career and life!" is a better approach to improving morale and, consequently, productivity.

Unfortunately, most employees, lacking a structured framework to assess their motivational needs, do not have the insight or a clear understanding of their needs, even if they were asked.

One of the biggest problems in providing an incentive and reward program that accommodates differing motivational needs is identifying individual employee needs and keeping up with those needs as they change over time due to personal life-style changes, professional development and growth needs, and career ambitions.

It is clear from the interview results that our workforce is increasingly embracing an organizational culture that provides opportunities to better balance their professional life with their personal life. We must address this issue as an organization or we face the prospect of continuing to see high employee turnover and decreases in morale and productivity.

Page 7: Management Report Example

Recommendations and Justification

In our review of currently available psychometric tools that address motivational needs, we found a few that have a motivation component. Only one tool focused specifically on providing a means to help our employees and managers better understand and communicate their workplace motivational needs. This tool, Motivator, available on the Internet, provides a framework to help people gain insight and understanding about what motivates them.

We strongly recommend Motivator as the tool we need to improve workplace communication, job satisfaction and productivity, as amplified below.

In addition to conducting research, identifying problem areas, and recommending solutions for improving employee morale and productivity, this assignment included providing justification for the recommendations. The following addresses anticipated questions along with in-depth, detailed responses to justify our recommendations.

1. How does the Motivator® tool work?

Motivator is an interactive, Internet-based tool that presents the participant with the challenge of distributing or sorting 50 work-related statements into varying degrees of desirability or undesirability. Examples of statements are: *Interesting work, Salary based on performance, Being a team player, Suitable work facilities, Freedom to plan work,* etc.

When the participant completes the sort process, the system processes the distribution into 10 different Motivation Categories that are comparatively rated on a 10-point scale where 10 is the highest rating. The result is a graphic bar chart display with a thorough description of each Motivation Category. Motivation

Page 8: Management Report Example

Categories include: *Responsibility, Work Relationships, Compensation, Advancement,* etc.

The participant then receives a detailed analysis of how his or her sort of work-related statements are used to score and rank his or her Motivational Categories. In other words, if the participant's primary motivation category is *Achievement* or *Work Itself* there is a detailed explanation of how that was derived by Motivator.

Subsequently, the system guides the participant through a series of questions related to specific statements that are of importance to him or her and prompts for input regarding each of the statements.

Then the system presents an interpretation of the Motivation Profile to the participant along with the option to create and print his or her individual comprehensive **Motivator Profile Report.**

The entire process takes most participants about 30 minutes to complete. An example of a completed Motivation Profile is available online at www.motivatortool.net.

To access the example Motivation Profile:

1. Click on the ACCESS Button.
2. Under Account Login, enter the following: Username: **Motivator,** Password: **Profile.**
3. Click on the Login Button. That takes you to the Motivator Command Center where you can follow directions to access the Motivation Profile example.

2. *What about the cost of Motivator®?*

The fee for an individual motivation profile, including the profile analysis and a comprehensive 16 page report is $20.

Page 9: Management Report Example

Volume discounts are available for companies and other organizations along with "branding" and accessibility via corporate intranet facilities. Depending upon the needs of an organization, Motivator fees are based on a variable, or "per use" basis, with no large fixed-fee costs. Our Company qualifies for a 20% discount based on an estimated number of uses for approximately 500 people.

The costs associated with Motivator are quite favorable compared to other psychometric tools such as the MBTI (*Myers-Briggs Type Indicator*) for identifying personality preferences and DiSC (*Dominant, Influencing, Steady, Conscientious*), a 4 quadrant tool for identifying behavior styles and personality types.

3. Do employees consider their motivational profiles confidential?

Respect for individual privacy and confidentiality is of utmost importance to our Company and to the Motivator organization. Motivator operates in a certified secure environment.

Additionally, we have our policies and procedures to protect the privacy of our employees. Given the prior substantial use of Motivator to create several thousand profiles with dozens of companies and organizations, it turns out that very few people insist on keeping their motivation profiles confidential.

From a practical perspective, it turns out that confidentiality is rarely a concern. Organizations experienced with using Motivator have learned that very few people insist on keeping their motivation profiles confidential. In fact, most people want to share their motivational needs, especially with someone who is in a position to understand and facilitate meeting those needs. Why? The best way for them to get the rewards that are

Page 10: Management Report Example

most meaningful to them is for management to know what "rings their bell."

Nonetheless, the Motivator organization recommends voluntary, not mandatory, use of the tool. They further encourage that if someone is reluctant to share his or her profile, or wishes to keep it confidential, to respect and honor those wishes.

4. Do motivational needs change overtime?

Yes, motivational needs do change over time. Unlike personality and problem solving styles, what motivates people does indeed change. For example, compensation may be a strong motivator early in one's career and then when that need is satisfied, it may be displaced by recognition or perhaps work itself. Compensation could again become a stronger motivator if expense demands increase such as the need for college tuition for children or a need to accommodate parents.

The appeal of Motivator is that it is a tool that can provide both current and future motivational profiles and can be revised at minimal expense at any time.

5. What makes the Motivator® tool so effective?

The effectiveness of Motivator lies in its ability to facilitate interactive development of a motivation profile that defines the work environment a person considers optimal for productivity, harmony, and success in the workplace.

Motivator draws from all the key motivational theories—from Maslow, to Herzberg, Skinner, Vroom, and Locke. Further, it assimilates all the motivational theories and condenses them to enable managers to find out what it is that employees need or want in a work relationship from a motivation standpoint.

Page 11: Management Report Example

If a manager wants an employee to be productive, he or she needs to create a social contract that says to the employee, "you give me what I need from you and in return, I will give you the incentives and rewards that you want." A manager needs to make sure that he or she is consistent in using that approach. Since this is the fundamental philosophy behind Motivator, it is a very effective tool for facilitating effective working relationships and the key reason for recommending Motivator for our Company.

Summary

Thank you for this important and challenging assignment. While it is unfortunate that we needed this assignment in the first place, we are pleased that we were able to uncover the root cause of our increasing turnover, decreasing morale and productivity through the honesty and candor of the survey results. It turns out that our current incentive and reward program does not satisfactorily meet the motivation needs of our workforce.

After a thorough investigation of currently available tools, we recommend using Motivator to: 1) provide an effective solution for improving communication, job satisfaction and productivity of our workforce by identifying individual motivational needs; 2) revise our current incentive and reward program to better meet those needs.

Motivator is a cost-effective tool that accurately identifies motivational needs including the changing of needs over time. It addresses confidentiality concerns and facilitates open discussion and understanding of employees' desired rewards.

Page 12: Management Report Example

May we have your approval to move forward with an initiative to:

1. Purchase use of the Motivator tool to identify our employees' motivational needs?
2. Establish a diverse focus group to revise our incentive and reward program, aligning those needs with the goals and objectives of our Company?

Be Careful of What You Put in Writing

Additionally, we must deal with a significant difference between interpersonal and written communication. While it seems obvious, it is frequently forgotten. Can you guess what it is?

The written word *communicates and documents*. What does that really mean? Written communication tends to be filed away and stored. Someone other than the intended reader may see it months or even years later and interpret it completely differently.

For example, if you took over a job at a new Company, would you be inclined to review recent as well as past correspondence that was left by your predecessor? In so doing, you would be reading communication by staff members that you perhaps had not even met. What could be the danger in that? Could you possibly develop some unfair preconceived opinions about other people in the organization?

Are you more impressed by clear, effective communication than by prose that is difficult to understand and filled with grammatical errors? We are often making our first impression from a letter or document written years ago. What is the practical implication of this? Always keep in mind that what you put in writing for one reader may well be read by other unintended readers especially if it is communicated on the Internet. It can come back to haunt you even years later.

The bottom line is to always be careful with all of your communication—especially when you put it in writing.

When Writing, Be Nice

Written communication plays a documentation role; therefore, it has a special application—but first the caveat. Something negative put into writing generally comes across as much harsher than if it is explained verbally. Why? As explained in the beginning of this chapter, it is because we lose our NON-verbal communication tools of:

- ➢ Voice inflection
- ➢ Body language
- ➢ Being able to read and adapt to the audience
- ➢ Using a query, for instance, if someone seems to be getting upset

Another point is that something negative in writing is *out there* and you cannot take it back. It can be out there for a long time and someone can go through the file, pick it up a year from now and get hurt or angry all over again.

Are There Exceptions?

Is there an exception to every rule? For example, let's say there is a negative situation, such as poor performance from an employee. As illustrated in the section, "Can You Fire Someone Just by Asking Questions?" in Chapter 10, it makes sense to do some interactive probing to make sure we have an understanding of the true facts for a particular situation.

For example, if I were to send an email to one of my employees, Bob, saying; "You've been behind on your projects lately and it's causing serious problems," then later discover that Bob's wife has been diagnosed as terminally ill which is contributing to his performance problems, I might want to take it back!

A better approach is to combine interpersonal with written communication. Find an appropriate time to ask, "Bob, how is everything going with you? Do you think you are meeting project schedules?" As Bob explains his personal problem, you learn the context of the situation and can take a more appropriate approach.

On the other hand, suppose this conversation occurs: "Bob, how are things going with your project schedules?" Bob replies, "Well, I've been late recently." My next question could be, "What do you think is causing this and how can we remedy it?" Bob responds with, "I've just had a lot of work, and I need to plan better and work extra hours if needed." This conversation could be followed up with written communication to document it for future reference in case the problem does not get resolved.

For example, you could send a memorandum saying: "Thanks for meeting to discuss the project schedule issues. I appreciate your acknowledgment of the lateness problem as well as your thoughts on remedying it. Please implement your ideas on better planning and working extra hours. We can assess progress again at the end of the quarter. Please let me know if I can be of assistance as you strive to get projects on schedule."

What is the primary advantage of interpersonal communication prior to written? You have the opportunity to adapt to the context of a particular situation. When Bob reads the written communication, he recalls the non-verbal attributes of the conversation. Simultaneously, you create a written audit trail, in case the problem is ongoing.

Can you now see how to effectively use the verbal communication models to better make your point in written communication—whether an email, memo, letter or report?

Becoming a World Class Communicator

Effective communication is at the core of all relationships—both personal and business. Unintended communication breakdowns damage or cause many relationships to fail.

By learning and using the verbal and non-verbal communication models presented in this book, you can make your point in a convincing, non-argumentation manner in workplace and personal situations and achieve mutually beneficial results that build lasting relationships.

This page is for taking notes and jotting down practice scripts.

This page is for taking notes and jotting down practice scripts.

Cut out the Communication Flow Diagram to use as a quick reference when first practicing with the Verbal Models.

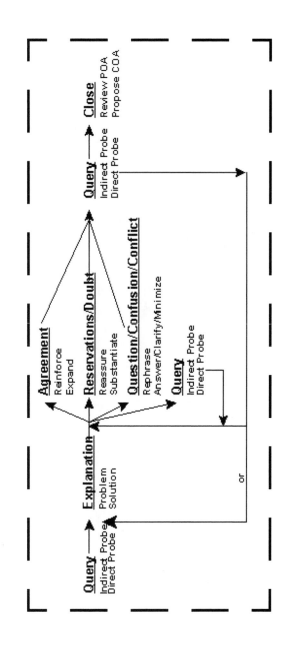